3 4143 100 8 3753

D0505260

WITHDRAWN
FOR SALE

Life A

DEAD

Life Among the
DEAD

WARRINGTON BOROUGH COUNCIL	
34143100183753	
Bertrams	30/11/2009
AN	£8.99
WAR	

HAY HOUSE

Australia • Canada • Hong Kong • India
South Africa • United Kingdom • United States

Names and identifying details of some of the people
portrayed in this book have been changed.

Published and distributed in the United Kingdom by:
Hay House UK Ltd, 292B Kensal Rd, London W10 5BE. Tel.: (44) 20 8962 1230;
Fax: (44) 20 8962 1239. www.hayhouse.co.uk

Published and distributed in Australia by:
Hay House Australia Ltd, 18/36 Ralph St, Alexandria NSW 2015.
Tel.: (61) 2 9669 4299; Fax: (61) 2 9669 4144. www.hayhouse.com.au

Published and distributed in the Republic of South Africa by:
Hay House SA (Pty), Ltd, PO Box 990, Witkoppen 2068.
Tel./Fax: (27) 11 467 8904. www.hayhouse.co.za

Published and distributed in India by:
Hay House Publishers India, Muskaan Complex, Plot No.3, B-2, Vasant Kunj, New
Delhi – 110 070. Tel.: (91) 11 4176 1620; Fax: (91) 11 4176 1630.
www.hayhouse.co.in

Distributed in Canada by:
Raincoast, 9050 Shaughnessy St, Vancouver, BC V6P 6E5. Tel.: (1) 604 323 7100;
Fax: (1) 604 323 2600

© Lisa Williams, 2009

The moral rights of the author have been asserted.

All rights reserved. No part of this book may be reproduced by any mechanical,
photographic or electronic process, or in the form of a phonographic recording; nor
may it be stored in a retrieval system, transmitted or otherwise be copied for public
or private use, other than for 'fair use' as brief quotations embodied in articles and
reviews, without prior written permission of the publisher.

The author of this book does not dispense medical advice or prescribe the use of any
technique as a form of treatment for physical or medical problems without the advice
of a physician, either directly or indirectly. The intent of the author is only to offer
information of a general nature to help you in your quest for emotional and spiritual wellbeing. In the event you use any of the information in this book for yourself,
which is your constitutional right, the author and the publisher assume no responsibility for your actions.

A catalogue record for this book is available from the British Library.

ISBN 978-1-84850-087-7

Printed and bound by CPI Bookmarque, Croydon CR0 4TD.

Photo by Kevin Harris

My mentor, Merv Griffin

This book is dedicated to the legendary Merv Griffin, my own personal angel.

I first met Merv in June 2004 and never imagined that this wonderful, warm, caring man was about to change the course of my entire life. He was there for me every step of the way, guiding me along and supporting me, and I will never forget his generosity.

Merv passed away in August 2007 while I was working on this book, but he was present while I continued to work on it, and I assure you that he's with me still. Merv once said that even after he was gone he would continue to executive produce my show, and he has kept his word.

I want to thank you, Merv, from the bottom of my heart, for everything you've done for me and my family.

We love you and feel blessed to have known you.

Contents

Lisa, age two and a half

chapter 1

The Uninvited

I was three years old when I saw dead people for the very first time.

We were living in a flat in Birmingham, in Central England, our family's first real home, and I soon discovered that we weren't alone. Strange faces, balloonlike and oddly translucent, came floating in and out of the walls of my room, and because they were slightly blown up, as if filled with air, they seemed a little clownish. But there was nothing funny about them.

I went to tell my parents. "There are people in the walls of my room," I said.

"What people?"

"I don't know. All sorts of people."

Mom took me by the hand and walked me back. "Where?" she said.

"Well, they're gone *now*, but they were here a minute ago."

"You're making this up."

"No, I'm not."

"Who are they, then?"

"I don't know. Just people, some of them look like clowns."

"Clowns? It's just your imagination! Go to bed."

The next night, the faces were back. I went into the lounge and *refused* to return to my room. My parents were just about to go to bed and, unhappy at the prospect of another sleepless night, my father gave me an angry look and marched off. "If you want to stay on the sofa all night, that's fine, but I'm going to sleep."

I stared at him, even as he switched off the lights and left me in the dark, but feeling guilty, he returned a few minutes later and found me sitting there, still staring. I hadn't moved.

"Why are you such a defiant child?" he said.

"What's 'defiant'?" I asked, scowling.

He picked me up, carried me to bed, plunked me down, and stormed off without saying a word.

For the next few months, the drama continued, sometimes two or three nights a week. An endless array of faces, ghostly and insubstantial, would emerge from the walls, study me for a moment or two, even try to grab at me at times, then just as suddenly dematerialize. Some of them actually addressed me, but I could never make out what they were saying, and they scared me.

"What do they say?" Mom asked.

"I dunno, but one of them comes through the lightbulb and tries to yank my hair."

"Comes through the lightbulb?"

"I just see her arm."

"How do you know it's a girl?"

"Dunno," I said, shrugging my shoulders. "I just don't think boys pull hair."

Exasperated, my parents finally moved me into the spare bedroom, but the faces were back that very night. Bony old men. Angelic boys. Old ladies. Thin girls with pinched cheeks. I went to get my mother, to show her, but by the time we returned, they had disappeared.

"There is nothing there," she said. "It's just your imagination. Go to sleep."

After tucking me in, she curled up in bed with me and stayed until I fell asleep.

There were nights when I would lie in bed scared, begging the uninvited visitors to leave me alone. I'd bury my head under the covers, thinking they would go away if I couldn't see them. And other nights I'd shout at them, "Go away! This is my room! I don't like you!"

My parents were concerned, but they thought I just had a vivid imagination. This was thirty years ago and therapy wasn't an option in my family. We never really showed emotion, and seeing a therapist wasn't even in the realm of possibility, so they dealt with my complaints by ignoring them. And it worked! Whenever I mentioned the faces, they would roll their eyes and continue what they were doing. In time, I stopped talking about them altogether, and soon enough—taking a cue from my parents—I began to ignore the spirits. They still came, of course, but they didn't bother me anymore.

I also began to ignore my parents—or at least that's the way it appeared. "Lisa! I'm talking to you! Are you listening to me?"

I would look up from my perch on the floor, where I was playing. "What?"

"What is wrong with you? Are you deaf?"

As it turned out, I was hard of hearing. I had compensated for this defect, unknowingly, by reading lips, which I guess I'd been doing ever since words first began to make sense to me. If I didn't look at a person directly, I couldn't really make out what they were saying to me—which was the same problem I had with my nightly visitors.

When I was five, Mom took me to Birmingham Children's

Hospital, where we were told that the tubes to my ears were almost completely blocked. The surgeon cleaned them out and removed my tonsils and adenoids for good measure, and when I awoke I could hear just as well as the next person. This was wonderful indeed, but—even better—every afternoon at three the nurses showed up with big scoops of ice cream. I loved ice cream so much I didn't want to leave the hospital!

In the summer, I would play in the big grassy area in front of our building, waiting for the ice cream man to show up. When I heard him coming, I would shout up to the third-floor balcony, "MOM!!!" Moments later, a fifty-pence piece would come sailing off the balcony, tumbling end over end. I would watch like a hawk to see where it landed, then I'd grab it and hurry off to meet the ice cream man.

Except for the haunting faces, life was great, especially now that we had a home of our own. My mother, Lorraine, stayed home in those days to care for me, and my father, Vic, worked as a self-employed contractor. Previously, we had lived with my father's parents, Jack and Josie, in West Heath, Birmingham, They had a two-bedroom house with a lovely, long garden, and I'd run up and down the entire length of it tirelessly, urging my grandparents to look at me. My grandfather would always be out there, tending to his plants, and he always humored me by looking over.

During the cold winters, I would have snowball fights with my dad, then we'd go inside and huddle around the fireplace with the rest of the family. I especially remember Tuesday nights, because every Tuesday, without fail, Mom and Nanny Josie would go off to play bingo at the local bingo hall. I started to call my nan Bingo Nanny.

In 1976, two years after we moved into our own home, my brother Christian came along. I still remember watching my mother carry this bundled little creature into the house for the first time. I hoped his constant screaming would scare off the spirits, but they didn't seem to be troubled by the crying; in fact, they weren't even vaguely interested in him.

Eventually, tiring of hearing me complain about the visitors, my parents had me switch rooms with Christian, and my mother's mother, Frances Glazebrook, paid to have the room redone. She and my parents chose Holly Hobbie wallpaper. Holly Hobbie was a little girl in a blue chintz bonnet, and she was supposed to personify childhood innocence. She was cute but she had these eyes that freaked me out at night. Now I had to deal with the spirits *and* with Holly Hobbie, staring at me.

In September 1977, I went off to nursery school. I was four at the time. Mom took me the first day, but the second day I was sent off to join the parade of children who made their way down the path every morning, past our building. I tried to be brave about it, but when I got there, I saw that most of the other kids in my class had arrived with their mothers, and that one of them had actually brought flowers for the teacher. I was so upset that I ran all the way home in tears to find my mom. "You're supposed to walk me to school," I said, blubbering. "And you forgot to bring flowers for the teacher."

We went outside and picked a few flowers, and Mom walked me back to school. I gave the flowers to the teacher, who was most appreciative, and settled in. I enjoyed school, but I was shy, and quite insecure. I had a hard time making friends, and the year proved somewhat lonely for me.

I'd gotten used to the visitors by then, but I still huddled under the covers from time to time, trying to ignore them. One evening, just as Mom called me to dinner, a distinguished-looking gentleman, nicely dressed in a brown jacket and matching trousers, appeared in the hallway and followed me to the dining room. It was a *whole* gentleman, not just a face or an arm.

"Don't eat your peas," he said.

"Huh?" I said.

"Don't eat your peas or you'll die."

My dad looked at me, perplexed. "Are you talking to one of your imaginary friends?" he asked.

"He's not imaginary," I said, pointing in his direction. "Can't you see him?"

He looked toward the spot I'd indicated, but saw nothing. "Who?"

"*There!* He's standing right *there!*"

"Don't eat your peas," the man repeated.

"Okay," I answered.

"I don't see anyone," Dad said.

"He's telling me not to eat my peas or I'll die."

My parents thought I was making it up because I didn't like peas, which I *didn't,* but the man was standing there, clear as day. They didn't believe it, but they gave up trying to talk sense to me. "Okay," Mom said, rolling her eyes. "Don't eat your peas."

I recently found out that my dad's great uncle always had pie, chips, and peas for lunch, and one day—a few years before I was born—he choked on a pea and died. To this day I have a terrible phobia of peas.

My favorite food at the time—the only food I cared for, really—was a cheese sandwich. Not even *grilled,* mind you; just two slices of bread with cheese and salad cream, which is like mayonnaise with horseradish.

One night, there was a tomato on my plate and the man was back. "Don't eat the tomato, either. You could choke. Avoid anything with pips."

"Okay," I said.

"What?" Mom said.

"I wasn't talking to you," I said.

"There's nobody there," she said.

"He's right there, Mom! He told me not to eat the tomato."

"No, he's not. It's just a ploy to avoid eating your vegetables. He's just like your monkey."

She had a point there. I had an imaginary monkey, whom I'd named "Monkey." I took him everywhere with me because he was good company and nice to chat with. He was a *talking* monkey. We were inseparable. If I ever forgot him, I moaned until we went back to the house to get him.

The following year, when I was five, we moved into a council house in Tillington Close, in Redditch, Worcestershire, twenty miles south of Birmingham, and that's where I lived until I turned nineteen. It was a mid-terraced, red-brick house with three bedrooms, a dining room, and a spacious living room, and there was a huge patch of grass out front that we shared with our immediate neighbors.

I was so excited to move. I chose my new room, hoping to leave my visitors behind at the old flat. But the faces were back the very first night—different faces. I was determined to start afresh, so I ignored them. I started at the Ten Acres First School, which was close by, and on my very first day I made friends with Samantha Hodson, who remains a close friend to this day. I was a little behind at school, mostly on account of my deafness, and I couldn't read and write as well as the other kids, but I caught up quickly and grew to love the place. I loved sports and music and I especially loved singing; I was delighted when I was asked to join the choir.

There was a girl in my year and for some reason, I became very competitive with her until we left school at eighteen. Her name was Helen Waugh, and she could play the recorder and even read music, which impressed me to no end—and made me very jealous (even though I liked her). Motivated by her superior skill, I learned to play the recorder and read music. Then she took up the violin, and I took up the violin. This went on for years and years, and because of Helen, I now have varied taste in music. I also sang, danced, and played sports; my days were so full that I fell into bed exhausted every night, with absolutely no time for my otherworldly visitors.

On Saturdays, my little brother and I would usually go round to visit my maternal grandmother, Frances, and my grandfather, Jack, at their home in Bartley Green. My cousins would often be there, and we'd dance and run around and shoot tin cans in the garden with an air rifle. Sundays after lunch we'd go visit my father's parents, Jack and Josie, and the adults would always get into long debates about Margaret Thatcher, the British Prime Minister, who—if you asked my granddad—was ruining the country. There were no cousins here because my father was an only child, so in a way it felt more special. It was just me and Christian, and since he was still an infant, I got most of the attention.

On Sunday nights, we always got home late, and I'd often pretend to be asleep so that my dad would wrap me in his arms and carry me to bed. On one such night, genuinely exhausted, I had a very vivid, scary dream. In the morning, still rubbing the sleep from my eyes, I arrived at the breakfast table and dropped into my seat. "Do you remember those dogs that mauled me?" I asked.

"What dogs?"

"I don't know what kind they were. Just three big, black and brown dogs.

"Don't be silly," my mother said. "You've never been mauled by dogs."

"Yes I have," I said.

"Quiet down and eat your breakfast. It's just your imagination."

"But I know it happened!" I protested. "Why are you telling me it didn't?"

Once again they ignored me, which only upset me more. I knew it had only been a dream, but somehow it was *real*. In the dream I was maybe three or four years old, with long, wispy, platinum blond hair. My *actual* hair was thick and light brown and cut in the shape of a bowl, tapering inward along the sides of my face—we used to call that a Purdey—but years earlier I'd had hair just like the girl in the dream. I was only seven at the time, and I knew nothing about past lives or reincarnation, but I was convinced the dream was real.

The little girl was not me in this life, but she felt like a version of me. "There were three big dogs," I insisted. "And they were chewing me. I could feel their teeth sinking into my skin."

My mom tutted and rolled her eyes.

"But it's true! It really happened! I even heard a woman screaming, and it might have been you."

Mom gave me that look: *Here we go again.*

"I'm not making it up!" I insisted. "It really happened!"

"Finish your breakfast and get ready for school," my father said.

I couldn't understand why they didn't believe me, especially since my mother's mother, Frances, experienced visions that came true and saw dead people too. Also, my father's mother, Josie, read tea leaves and often spoke of odd visions, vivid dreams, and strange sensations. Then again, I'd often heard my dad scoff about these "so-called gifts," saying he didn't believe a word of it. He didn't believe much of anything, to be honest. Religion, for starters. I went to a Church of England school, but neither of my parents attended church. "I don't believe in God or Heaven or anything beyond this life," my father used to say. "When you're dead, you're dead."

My mother was more open, and she often told me that she felt that something was in store for all of us after we passed away. She didn't think God or Jesus had much to do with it, however, and she certainly didn't spend much time worrying about it.

I remember once asking my parents why I hadn't been christened, like most of my friends, and my dad was pretty blunt in his response: "Because I don't believe and I'm not a hypocrite," he said. "If you want to do it, then do it, but you'll follow through by going to church every Sunday. It's up to you."

I had plenty to keep me busy on Sundays, so I decided against it. But it wasn't based on lack of faith. I was a child and I simply didn't know what to believe, and it was clear that my parents weren't going to be particularly helpful in helping me decide.

Just before I turned eight, my maternal granddad passed away, and my Nan Frances had to adjust to life as a widow. Almost immediately after the funeral, which, for some reason, I was not allowed to attend, she began going to the local Spiritualist Church, something she had denied herself when her husband was alive, since he was another staunch nonbeliever. It was evident almost from the start that she had a gift, and before long she was performing public demonstrations. Her favorite venue was the Harborne Healing Centre, a spiritualist organization in a suburb of Birmingham, where she would communicate with people who had passed over, sharing their messages with their loved ones. She started doing private readings at her home, and she was so good that before long she was traveling around the world to read for some of her wealthier clients. Because of this I took to calling her Airplane Nanny.

Airplane Nanny with one of her many friends

From time to time, I would hear my parents talking about her. My father was dismissive, of course, but my mother was curious and more than a little impressed. Frances had segued effortlessly into the next chapter of her life, and she was adjusting quite nicely.

I never asked about any of this, of course, because I somehow felt the subject was off-limits, but I loved visiting her. She wasn't your typical grandmother, like my dad's mom, who baked cakes and played with us and made lovely dinners. No, Airplane Nanny was glamorous; she had no interest in playing games. She had her hair done every week, loved jewelry, and really loved to laugh. She had a wild, almost bawdy laugh, and when she started you couldn't help laughing too—even if you didn't understand the joke.

She was also thoroughly modern. She always had the best phone, or the latest answering machine, or the newest VCR. But she liked old things too. She had a collection of brasses that had once been worn by Shire horses, those great big draught horses that were once used to haul beer from the breweries. She kept them along with a huge, shiny brass plate above the fireplace; they were her pride and joy. She also had a brass doll with a little bell tucked up inside its skirt, which sat on the mantel, and I never got tired of ringing the bell—though everyone else did.

Inevitably, I began to cross paths with some of her clients, and I'd be told to make myself scarce. "You'll have to go play outside," she'd say. "I have someone coming to see me."

"What is it these people come see you about?" I finally asked her. I couldn't understand what these people wanted from her, or why she never answered the constantly ringing phone.

"I'm clairvoyant, I do readings," she explained. "I talk to their loved ones who are in spirit and am able to look into the future."

"Oh," I said. I didn't think to ask her how she did this, but I suspected it had something to do with the cards she kept on the mantel. I had asked about the cards once before, and she had been quick to respond: "You must never touch them. These are very special cards, they are not playing cards, and they're not for you. Not yet, anyway."

When I was nine, I had another very vivid dream. "Did one of our houses burn down when I was little?" I asked my parents.

"Why would you say something like that?" Mom asked.

"I had a dream last night. I was surrounded by fire. But I woke up before I burned to death."

"I hope you don't talk about these things outside the house," my dad said with his usual dismissiveness.

"I don't," I said. But that was only partly true. I did share some of them with Sam Hodson, my best friend, because I knew she wouldn't tell.

"It didn't actually feel like a dream," I went on. "It felt like it was really happening to me."

"You have an overactive imagination," Mom said.

"I can't have," I said. "My teacher is always telling me to be more imaginative."

Tuesday after school I usually went to Sam's house, played, and had dinner, staying until 7:30, and Thursdays she came to mine and did the same. Occasionally, we had sleepovers. One night we were at my house, and we were talking about my grandmother, Frances, who was beginning to get quite a reputation around Birmingham. "Do you think you have the gift?" Sam asked me.

"The gift? I don't know that it's a gift. It's just something she does. She reads the cards and tells people what she sees."

"It's a *gift*, I tell you," Sam insisted. "I heard it runs in families."

"Where did you hear that?"

"I'm not sure. On the telly, I think. Tell you what, let's see if you have the gift. Have you got a pack of playing cards?"

With uncertainty, I went off to fetch the cards and handed them to Sam. We sat cross-legged on my bed and Sam set the deck in front of her. She asked me to try to guess the cards, and she

Photo by Jack Williams

Lisa, Nan Josie, and Sam

peeled them off the deck, one at a time, and held them directly in front of her face.

"Ace of clubs," I said.

"Right!"

"Four of hearts."

"Right again!"

"Nine of diamonds."

"Oh my God!"

We went through all fifty-two cards, and I got every single one of them right. Sam was open-mouthed with shock. "Lisa!" she said. "That was incredible. I can't believe it. You have the gift! You have the gift!"

"No, I don't," I said. "Look behind you. The street light shone through the window and made the cards practically transparent. I can see right through them!"

Even after I showed her, she refused to believe me, thinking there was more to it, and she insisted we try something else. It was after ten o'clock, and I'd put out the lights because we were supposed to be asleep, but she looked around the darkened room and her eye settled on one of the bookshelves. I had a collection of about a hundred Ladybird books, which I loved. They weren't in any particular order, and in the dim light the titles were impossible to see.

"Tell you what," Sam said. "I'm going to touch the spine of one of the books, and you're going to tell me the title."

"Okay," I said. "But I'm going to need contact with the book through you."

"Why?"

"I don't know, someone just told me to do it." It was true: I'd heard a voice telling me how to make it work.

"You're weird," Sam said, looking at me like I was crazy, but still smiling.

"I know, you keep telling me," I said.

Sam reached for my hand with her right hand, then rested the index finger of her left hand on the spine of one of the books. I started to see the image of a book I'd read at least a hundred times. "*The Princess and the Pea*," I said.

She pulled the book out of the shelf and brought it near the window, where there was just enough ambient light to make it out. "Oh my God!" she said. "You're right!"

We tried again, and again it worked, and we tried twice more, and both times I got the titles right. We freaked out. Then the door to the room opened, startling us. It was Mom, alerted by our girlish screaming. "What's going on here? You're supposed to be asleep."

"Mom! Guess what happened!" I said, and I told her, breathless with excitement. She listened attentively, waited until I was done, then studied me solemnly and said, "It's time for bed now, but I think you need to have a little talk with your grandmother."

Sam and I lay awake for a long time, but we didn't talk because we were both too excited—and a little scared.

I went to see Frances that weekend, and I repeated the story. "I'm not surprised," she said. "You're a very special child."

"I bet all nans say that," I replied.

"Maybe, but this is different. You are special."

"What does that mean, exactly?"

"You'll find out more when the time comes," she said with a smile, then turned and indicated the Tarot cards on the mantle. "Remember what I said about those cards. You mustn't touch them—or the ouija board, either, for that matter—you are not ready," she said.

"Why? Will something bad happen?" I asked.

"No, you're just not ready," she said, patting the back of my hand. "You might attract spirits you can't deal with. But don't worry about it. We'll talk more about this when you're older." Suddenly I understood that my little visitors were spirits trying to communicate with me.

That same week, Sam decided to tell the other kids at school about me, and how I'd named four book titles in a row. "She has a gift," she said, laughing, and I could feel my face turning red. "Lisa's weird!"

I wasn't offended—she was actually quite impressed, and she meant it in a loving way—but I suggested that it was probably a series of lucky guesses. "No, no," she said. "You're different than us. You're special."

I had shared many things with Sam, but I had never told her about the faces, or about the dreams. Or, more recently, about other "feelings" I picked up during the course of the day. I knew if there was going to be a test before I even walked into class, for example. Or if one of the students was going to go home sick. I even remember feeling sorry for a boy who sat next to me in class, not knowing why, and two days later he showed up at school with a cast on his broken arm. Sometimes I knew the phone was going to ring and who'd be calling. "Dad, Airplane Nanny's gonna call for Mom."

A moment later, the phone would ring, and my dad would look at me like I was crazy, then go off to answer it.

The odd part was, my friend Sam was much more of a believer than I was. I wasn't even all that interested in my *so-called gift*, to be completely honest. It made me self-conscious. I wanted to be like other girls, not different, so once again I dealt with it by trying to ignore it. I ignored the faces that came through the walls. I ignored the chatter in my head. I ignored the vivid dreams. I ignored the quirky feelings I picked up as I went about my day. I even ignored the pains in my legs that kicked in whenever something bad was going to happen. Instead, I poured my energy into dancing, swimming, gymnastics, music, and singing, and I enjoyed myself, but a little voice in my head kept repeating the same thing: *This isn't where your talents lie.* Alas, in my quest for normalcy I ignored that little voice, too.

I did well in school, if not spectacularly, and I had friends, but I wouldn't say I was immensely popular. To tell the truth, I was a bit lonely as a child. I'd go about my day at school, then walk home mid-afternoon, let myself into house, and potter about aimlessly till my parents came home, which was seldom before six o'clock. (Mom was working as a seamstress by this time, and Dad was still in construction.) That's why Tuesdays and Thursdays were my favorite days, because I got to spend them with Sam: Tuesdays at her house, with her lovely parents, Sue and Ray, and her brother, Darren, and Thursdays at mine, because Thursday was Mom's day off.

By the time I turned eleven, England was in the middle of a recession, and my parents were working harder than ever, trying to make ends meet. Dad usually worked six days a week, and his spare time was spent on the golf course, and Mom only had Thursdays and Sundays off. As a result, my brother and I began to spend weekends with Jack and Josie, my grandparents. I missed my parents, and I longed to be closer to them, but there was nothing to be done about it.

That summer, and in many school holidays to come, I found myself spending long stretches with Nan and Granddad at their caravan—a mobile home—in Diamond Farm, Brean, which is in Somerset County, about an hour and a half from Birmingham. Those turned out to be the happiest holidays of my life.

My granddad would pack us into his red Austin Allegro, and we'd sing the entire way there. He had a great voice. We'd sing Barbra Streisand songs, or songs from the musical *Fame,* while Christian told us to be quiet and Nan gave us mints to stop the motion sickness. The excitement built with every passing mile, until we exited the motorway and pulled up to their home.

There were plenty of other kids who spent holidays in their own caravans, and we got to know all of them. Sometimes we'd go to the public pool in Burnham, nearby, or we'd walk the 365 steps that went up Brean Down, to look at the ancient battlements and the ocean, just beyond. We'd go in the water even though it was absolutely freezing.

At night, or when it was raining, I'd organize little parties or concerts, or get all the kids together to play cards. And every summer, in mid-July, a dozen city kids would show up with a religious organization called the Sunshine Group. They stayed for two whole weeks—easy to spot in their bright red shirts—and we'd play rounders with them, or cricket, or just lounge about the park getting to know each other.

Some days, I'd visit with Jack, a man my grandfather's age who spent his summer in the neighboring caravan. He was on a dialysis machine and went away every two days for treatment, but on good days he would play his violin. He had played violin with the Bristol Philharmonic, and with his help I got quite good on the violin myself.

Our caravan lacked proper plumbing, so we showered in the communal bathroom block, and we did the wash by hand. I often helped my grandmother. It was a little like traveling back in time, and I loved it.

It was there, at Diamond Farm, in the summer of 1986, that I had my first religious experience. I was thirteen at the time, and the Sunshine Group was back. This was the third summer I'd seen them, and the kids were always different, but the organizers were always the same. One of them asked me if I'd like to attend one of their meetings. I knew it was a religious thing, and I wasn't sure I should go, but I was curious, too—and a little voice in my head told me to go.

I told my nan I wanted to see what it was like. She was fine with it, and I found myself at the Village Hall, listening to some of the organizers talk about Christianity, and faith, and about the importance of welcoming God into our hearts. It was quite intense, but I was intrigued, and I liked the hymns we sang between speeches.

Toward the end of the evening, we were asked to bow our heads in prayer. I looked around and bowed my head, like everyone else. Then I heard a man's voice calling out from up front: "If you're visiting and want to welcome God into your life, please raise your hand."

I don't know exactly what happened to me, but my hand started to rise on its own. It was not a conscious decision. Even as it was happening, I was a bit taken aback. It was as if someone had attached a string to my wrist and was lifting it up without my consent.

"You can come forward," the man said.

I raised my head and looked up, and I noticed maybe six or seven other people making their way to the front of the hall. I got up and followed them. Up until this point, everyone else was praying, heads still bowed, but this must have been their cue to stop praying.

I felt everyone was looking at us, which no doubt they were, so

I was a little nervous. I found myself sitting next to a chubby blond boy with whom I'd played rounders earlier that day. I looked up. The organizer smiled at me. "You want to say a little prayer to the Lord?" he asked me.

I nodded, and closed my eyes and thought about what I wanted to say, but the organizer asked me to say it out loud. "Just say what's in your heart," he told me. "Whatever you feel is fine. Whatever comes to you will be right."

I clasped my hands in front of me and prayed: "I'm sorry if I've caused any problems for anyone, Lord. I'm going to try to be a good person. I am going to develop faith."

Even as I said these few words, I felt a little bad about it. I thought I was betraying my father, who was an atheist, and my mother, who was on the fence about religion. But a moment later the feeling passed—I wasn't doing anything wrong—and suddenly I was overwhelmed by good feelings. I don't know how to describe it other than to say that I felt as if this big empty hole inside me had suddenly been filled. I felt strangely *complete*.

I went back to my seat, smiling, almost giddy, and people kept coming by to congratulate me. There was something so genuine and warm about it that I was moved almost to the point of tears. I felt very close to everyone in that hall. I felt the world was suddenly beginning to make sense.

On my way back to the caravan, I was still giddy. I didn't know why I'd volunteered, or what exactly had happened, but I felt wonderful. I breathlessly described the entire experience to my nan. When I was done, she smiled but all she said was, "I'm glad you had a nice night," so I couldn't make out how she felt about it.

Still, I took it very seriously. The next day, the organizer gave me a pocket Bible, and he told me to read it now and then, and to make time for prayer. I read a little every day, and at night, when I went to bed, I always said a prayer. "Thank you for the day, God. Please keep me and my family safe."

When I returned home at the end of the summer, I told my mother that I wanted to be christened. She said she didn't have a problem with it, and that I should think about choosing my godparents. When I broached the idea with my father, however, he was less than enthused. "I'm okay with it, but as I said before, it's going to mean going to church every Sunday morning."

So we were back to that! "Well, who is going to come with me?" I asked.

"Ask your mother, you know how I feel about this."

I didn't want to ask my mom. She had enough to do, what with working five days a week in addition to the housework and looking after us. I went off to think about what he'd said. I didn't know if I believed in God either, but there was no denying the experience. I felt transformed—felt somehow *lighter*. I turned to my pocket Bible for some answers, but in a matter of days my interest in God and baptism and salvation began to wane. I was just a child, after all, and I guess I wasn't ready to give up my Sunday mornings.

Summer ended, and I started classes at Arrow Vale High School, where I began to think quite seriously about becoming a teacher, either in music or in physical education. My friend Sam was in the same school, but we drifted apart for a time because we were now in different classes. I was hanging out with three other girls—Zoe, Lynn, and another Lisa—and I was busy with music and sports. The psychic business was relegated to the background, but I still sensed things: A fight was about to break out in the schoolyard, a boy's father was going to die, a teacher would resign before the year was out.

In England, you can leave school at age sixteen; by then I had been at the school three years and all three of my new friends decided to leave. But I was determined to further my education and become a teacher, so I stayed on to do my A-levels, the exam necessary to qualify for university. Sam also stayed to do her A-levels, and I reconnected with her and another girl, called Andeline.

Out of the whole school, there were only about twenty of us studying for A-levels, and out of those twenty I was the only one pursuing music. One day, about a dozen of us were in the common room where we studied, and I slipped into the adjoining room to listen to *Dido and Aeneas,* an opera by Purcell. I was wearing headphones, and I could see part of the common room through the glass partition. I could see the lounge area, with its mismatched sofas, and the desks beyond, where everyone was busy studying. There was a small kitchenette off to one side, with a refrigerator and a coffeemaker and a microwave, but it wasn't in my field of vision.

Fifteen or twenty minutes later, I heard a little voice in my head telling me to switch off the music and go see what happened, so I removed my headphones and walked into the common room. The kids were all staring at me, and two or three of them were as white as ghosts.

"What happened to the glass?" I asked, even though I had no idea what I was referring to. "Who broke it?"

Sam glanced in the direction of the kitchenette, which was off to the right, not visible from where I stood, then turned again to face me. I went closer and peered around the corner and saw broken glass all over the floor. "Well?" I said, turning again to face them.

Sam pointed toward my pencil case, which I'd left on one of the empty desks. "Andeline needed some Typex," she said. "I knew you had some in your pencil case, so we all decided to try to move it by using our minds. We focused on moving your pencil case with our minds."

One of the other girls piped up: "That's when a glass exploded in the kitchen."

"We were just having a bit of fun," one of the guys said, almost apologetically. "You know, on account of how you used to have the gift." They'd all heard about that, of course, and they all knew about my grandmother, and at that moment they were all looking at me as if I'd had something to do with the exploding glass—something witchy.

"It's nothing," I said, acting as if I knew what I was talking about. "You created so much energy that the glass shattered. That's all."

They stared at me as if I had said something profound— profound and more than a little scary. Then two of the girls went into the kitchenette and cleared up the glass, and we never spoke of it again.

At the end of the school year, a big group of us went off to Blackpool for a day, to celebrate. It's a beach town in the north of England, very popular with tourists. We partied and drank too much and had loads of fun, and then we returned to our respective homes and went our separate ways. Some of my classmates went off to university, but unfortunately, despite my hard work, I didn't have good enough grades, so I spent the first few weeks of summer wondering what I was going to do with the rest of my life.

In the weeks and months ahead, I managed to see a good deal of Airplane Nanny, Frances, the psychic one. She had been a heavy smoker much of her life, and by the time she quit the cigarettes had taken their toll, but she still had days when she seemed as healthy and as energetic as ever. From time to time, for example, she would jet off to France, Spain, Mexico, and America—to "confer with clients," as she put it—and she always returned with handfuls of foreign coins for me, which I began to collect. When she was home, the phone was always ringing off the hook with people calling for appointments—she was so popular that she found it impossible to squeeze everybody in.

In fact, I'd often heard my mom talking to her friends about Frances's popularity. She said that she had once gone to a village fete, and that there had been a line of women around the block, desperate to have a reading with her. I remember being struck by this: that complete strangers would wait in line for hours for a chance to get a little advice and direction from my very own nan. I had no idea at the time that my life would soon take me in the same direction.

On those days when Nan was feeling under the weather, she'd put a hand-lettered sign on her front door that read: "Frances is not seeing anyone today. Please call back another day." People would knock anyway, and her son, Steven, who was living with her, had to drive them away. Uncle Steven was a nice man, but unfortunately had a drinking problem; Nan herself fancied the occasional drink. Whenever she traveled, she collected those little liquor bottles they used to sell on planes, and she always kept two or three in her purse so she could enjoy a little tot when she felt the need.

One day she caught me studying her Tarot cards, sitting in their usual place on the mantel. "What did I tell you about those!" she said. "You're not ready yet."

"I was just looking!" I said.

At that time, I had a part-time job as a waitress at the local golf club, where my dad had put in a good word for me, and shortly thereafter I took a second job at Graveneys, a sports shop in Redditch. On the occasional weekend, to get away, I'd borrow my mother's car and drive out to see my grandparents in Brean, and I'd spend the night with them in their caravan. That didn't last long, however, because I became friendly with Susan, one of the girls at Graveneys, and we discovered boys and nightclubs. At last, one of the joyous mysteries of life was revealed to me!

My parents were quite tolerant and would allow me to borrow the car as long as I had it back before Dad had to leave for work. Having access to the car gave me a wonderful sense of freedom, and many times I'd pull into the driveway after six a.m., cutting it fine. I'd run upstairs and jump into bed with all my clothes on, pretending to be asleep as if I had been there all night. I don't think I was fooling anyone. I'm sure they knew I had only just walked in, but they never said anything.

I would get as much sleep as I could, but I had to be out of bed by 8:30 to get to Redditch Town Centre, where I was now working full-time. Somehow I managed to survive on very little sleep, and the next night I was off to party all over again. But I was never late and I never missed work. I was very responsible.

Eventually, however, it all began to seem a little meaningless, and I decided that I really wanted to make something of my life. Without a proper degree, I would never become a school P.E. teacher, so I decided to do the next best thing and become a fitness instructor. I heard about an opening at the Pine Lodge Hotel, in Bromsgrove, the next town over, and I decided to take a drive out and pick up an application.

When I arrived I was quite impressed with the place. It had beautifully landscaped grounds, a fully equipped gym with state-of-the-art equipment, a large indoor pool, a sauna, and a steam room. When I subsequently went back for my interview, I was asked if I was a good swimmer, and I told them that I had in fact spent a summer qualifying as a swim instructor. That clinched it: The following week I gave notice at Graveney's, and the week after that I began at Pine Lodge.

Before long, I realized that I was in fact little more than a glorified cleaner. I'd assist members and hotel guests in the gym, posing as a personal trainer, and when there was no one around I arranged the changing rooms, emptied the laundry bins, and tidied up around the pool. I didn't mind it, though. I enjoyed meeting new people and having use of the gym. It had other advantages too. Before long I had made enough money to buy a car of my very own, a used Renault 19, a little four-cylinder job in a delightful faded gold color with matching interior. I loved it!

A few months into the job, I read an ad in the paper about a place in Trowbridge that was offering an intensive two-week course to qualify as an aerobics instructor. I sold the Renault at a surprising profit, even though I'd only had it for a short time, and bought a cheap Mini, brown in color. It was really zippy, so I took to calling it Chloe—The Flying Turd. I used the extra money to pay for the course, and when I got back to the Pine Lodge I felt eminently more qualified to put everyone through their paces.

Throughout this period, I had tried to ignore my psychic feelings, but there were a lot of quiet moments at work, and it seemed as if the gift was trying to manifest itself. A woman would come into the gym, for example, and I would somehow sense that she'd had an argument with her boyfriend, and before long I'd have her talking about it. Once I had a dream in which the hotel pool was empty, and lo and behold, the next day there was a problem with the draining system, and the workmen had to empty it and fix it. And whenever I went to the laundry room to deposit the used towels, I could feel the presence of a man I sensed had died there more than a hundred years ago. I had a feeling that he wanted to talk to me, and that all I had to do was listen, but I didn't really want to hear what he had to say. I wasn't all that interested in pursuing my *so-called gift*; I was more interested in normal life.

One evening I was at a nightclub called Celebrities in Stratford-on-Avon, about twenty minutes from home, where I would dance all night and have my usual Diet Coke—I never drank and didn't approve of drugs—when I met Paul. He was six feet tall, with thick, dark hair and a slim, athletic body, and he was my first love. He worked as a chef at a beautiful hotel in the Cotswolds, but he had dreams of opening a place of his own someday, and I loved his energy and his ambition. I remember thinking, *This is the man for me! I know it!* I immediately fell for him.

I introduced him to my parents, who loved him too, and he introduced me to his, who were absolutely lovely. Everything about the relationship was perfect, and for the better part of a year we were completely intertwined in each other's lives. We only existed as a couple, and I dreamt of our life together in years to come.

That summer we were invited to the wedding of one of his cousins, and we were excited to go. But when we arrived, for some reason I started having strange feelings about our future, and I sensed that Paul was keeping something from me. I decided to ask him, "Are you okay? I feel you have something to tell me."

"What do you mean?"

"I just have a feeling that something's not right. What is it? You know you can tell me anything."

"Don't be silly," he said. "If I had something to tell you, I'd tell you."

I let it go, but the feeling grew stronger, and a few days later he called and asked me if I wanted to meet him that night for a drink. This was weird because it was a Wednesday and we never saw each other on Wednesdays as he worked late, but he explained he had the night off. I was happy, but nervous; I knew something wasn't right. I confided in my friend and told her that I was sure Paul had something to tell me and I wasn't going to like it.

She said, "Stop worrying. You and Paul are going to grow old and wrinkly together. You are made for each other!"

As much as I wanted to believe her, I started to dread the evening to come.

We met at our usual pub and had a great time. I was feeling much more relaxed and told myself I was being silly for having those feelings of anxiety. It was a lovely night and he suggested a walk by the river. How romantic, maybe he has something he wants to say . . . or ask, I thought, with a secret hope that he had a ring in his pocket.

We walked hand in hand until he stopped and gestured to a bench overlooking the river. He looked me in the eyes and said, "Lisa, you are right. I do have something to tell you. It's about work, and it has been the hardest decision I have ever had to make in my life."

It turned out he'd been offered another job, in another county, and he'd already accepted, and he didn't see me as part of the plan. I was devastated. I cried for a week. I was in such bad shape that I couldn't go to work. Mom called in sick for me.

"I felt so connected to him, Mom," I said, blubbering away. "I feel like part of me has been ripped away. I thought he loved me."

"I know, I know," she said, trying to comfort me. "But things like this happen for a reason, you'll feel better in time."

Dad tried to comfort me too. "It's another brick in life's wall," he said. "You will have these heartaches, but the experience will just make you a stronger person."

I thought I understood what he was saying, that it was all part of life's lessons, but I never wanted to go through it again. It hurt too much, and I promised myself I would never allow myself to be hurt like that again.

Lisa and Christian at another karaoke bar

chapter 2

The Gift

When Paul moved away, we had a tearful farewell. I did get over him, eventually, but it was a long, difficult time, and I found myself hardened by the experience. Having decided I would never let another man hurt me, I closed my heart to relationships. I went out and danced my heart out. I started dating; sometimes I dated two or three guys at once. Mom used to joke with me—with a smirk on her face she'd say, just in case the phone rang, "Who do you want to speak to tonight?" There was an occasion when I went out to dinner with one guy and was home by 9 p.m. and then I was out with another guy for drinks at 10 p.m. that same night! I knew it wasn't right, that I was simply running away from emotion, but it's what I needed at the time. I was having fun and lots of it!

During this time, I started going to karaoke bars. I was a good singer, and I sang my heartache away with ABBA, Barbra Streisand, Tiffany, and the Pointer Sisters, among others.

There were still periods of time when I thought about Paul and we would chat on the phone, but I forced myself to move on, go out and have a bloody good time. I guess I was trying to become a stronger person.

One Sunday, one of my girlfriends came to fetch me on her motorbike, and we went off to see a show in Birmingham. But on the way back, for some reason we took a different route home, hit a patch of gravel, and I flew over the handlebars, landing, gracelessly, on all fours. I remember trying to get up but not being able to because of my injuries. Luckily some people witnessed the accident, stopped to help me into their car, and drove me to the hospital. Fortunately my friend was totally uninjured.

Because I worked out so much, the muscles in my legs had protected my knees. I hadn't broken anything, but my legs had to be bandaged, ankle to thigh, and I was given painkillers for my aching back. When I got home it was late. I wobbled like a bandaged mummy, somehow climbed the stairs, and clambered into bed without waking my parents. In the morning, Mom came to wake me.

"Lisa, come on, you are going to be late for—" she stopped in mid-sentence when she saw me lying there, stiff as a board.

"Err, I don't think I'll be going to work today, Mom!" I said, wincing in pain.

"The strange thing is, I somehow knew something was going to happen to you last night," she said, as she sat on my bed, sighing.

At the time, I remember thinking, *So she gets these feelings too. Just like Nan.*

I was off work for eight weeks, which gave me plenty of time to review my life, and it was a blessing in disguise because I honestly didn't like what I saw. I was nineteen years old and living at home. What was I waiting for? When was I going to begin to stand on my own two feet and finally move forward with my life? There was a massive world out there waiting to be explored!

One afternoon, still recuperating and feeling a bit sorry for myself, I was leafing through *Health and Fitness* magazine and came across an ad for an aerobics coordinator in Stevenage, Hertfordshire. It was a long way from home, but I wondered if that's what I needed—distance. I wrote a letter, applying for the job and describing my experiences, and ten days later I was invited to Stevenage for an interview. Because of my injuries, my mother drove and dropped me outside the building. I wore a long skirt to cover my bandages, but I still had walking sticks and was hobbling around like an old woman. I made my way into the Leisure Centre, as it was called, to meet the manager. She took one look at me—walking sticks and all—and said, "Well, I was going to ask you to teach a class while you were here, to get some idea of your abilities, but I can see that may be asking too much." And we both laughed.

We chatted for a while and I explained about the motorcycle accident. We seemed to click, and she asked me a lot of technical questions about the body, first aid and general fitness, all of which I knew, thanks to the course I'd taken in Trowbridge. I even offered to instruct an aerobics session despite my injuries. I think my determination must have impressed her. "Well," she said. "You're hired."

"Wow, thank you!" I said, trying not to sound too surprised.

"When can you start?"

"Two weeks," I said, because that's when the bandages were coming off.

"Two weeks it is, then." And with that she stood up and we shook hands and she walked me to the door. I hobbled off and climbed into Mom's car. "I got the job," I said, grinning. "I start in two weeks!"

"I don't know if I should be happy or sad," she said.

"Happy," I said, feeling excited. "I have a feeling my life is going to change in big ways. I don't know *how* exactly, but this is definitely the right move."

Two weeks later, I had found a room in a house in Stevenage, thanks to one of the girls from the Leisure Centre. I moved in and went off to work with great excitement and anticipation.

Working at the Centre was actually very pleasant, and I looked forward to the time I spent there. The Centre itself was huge. They had a hall for rock concerts and sporting events, a theater, a cafeteria, squash courts, a state-of-the-art gym, aerobics studio, and snooker tables. It felt like a genuine community, and I found it easy to make friends.

The offices were on the second floor, and that's where we went to collect our paychecks, but in fact I hated going up there. I felt a lot of spiritual activity, and on several occasions I saw the spirit of an older woman making her way up and down the corridors. She was transparent, outlined in a bright shade of white, and she would quite literally walk through the walls. When I worked the late shift, one of my duties was to wait for everyone to leave, then make my way around the ground floor, turning out all the lights, and it was here that I'd often hear children's muted voices in the near distance, punctuated by peals of happy laughter. This psychic activity seemed to become more intense, and I remember feeling very uncomfortable from the experience.

It had been a while since these feelings had bothered me—I actually mistakenly thought they were behind me for good—and I wasn't eager to acknowledge them. I'm not sure why exactly, but I remember thinking that I didn't want to get drawn in, suspecting that—if I did—it would be forever. The thought made me uncomfortable for reasons I didn't understand, and I decided that on my next visit home I would talk to my grandmother about it. She was in poor health at that point, but still battling on, and I knew she would have solid advice.

One night, after seeing the ghostly woman again, I decided to mention it to one of my colleagues, Marie. She said there had been rumors about the ghost woman who had walked the corridors for years, and that people assumed it was someone who had died in the building. I told her about the children's voices too, and I was amazed when she said that others had also heard the children playing. She didn't know the story behind it, but I wasn't the only one to report hearing voices.

A few nights later, Marie shared what I'd told her with one of her girlfriends, who was a big believer and wanted to meet me. We went out for a drink and the girlfriend wasted no time. "What do you see around me, then?" she asked.

"Nothing really," I said, then without thought said, "Oh, I do get a feeling that you're going to be moving house soon."

"What!" she said, laughing. "I love my house."

"I'm sorry, I don't know why I said that." And it was the truth, I still had no idea where these ideas were coming from.

Two weeks later, Marie told me that her friend had decided to leave her husband and that she was moving out of the house! I began to wonder if perhaps I really did have some kind of gift. I also wondered why I was fighting it. Maybe I could use it in a positive way, and maybe I was only delaying the inevitable.

From that point on, I made a conscious decision to be more open and try to develop my skills. A client came to the gym one morning, as happy as Larry, but I sensed things were not going well at home for him, and I mentioned it as tactfully as possible.

"How did you know?" he said. "We've told absolutely no one."

"I'm sorry," I said. "I didn't mean to pry."

"That's not it," he said. "I'm just trying to figure out how you knew. We've only just decided to get a divorce."

Another time, I met some people at a bar, and I whispered in one of the girls' ears, "Are you pregnant?"

"Of course not!" she said, looking at me strangely. "What makes you think that?"

"I don't know. I just get these feelings, that's all."

I ran into her in the same bar the following week, and when she saw me, she hurried over, practically trampling people in her excitement to get to me. "Lisa, you were right!" she said. "I *am* pregnant." I was as delighted as I was amazed.

One Friday night in yet another bar—God, I was doing a lot of bar-hopping back then!—a guy approached me and my girlfriend, vodka in hand, and barely said hello before I blurted out, "Your nan has just told me that your granddad's doing fine." I clasped my hand over my mouth as if that would pull the words back, but too late . . . they were out!

He spat his drink across the bar and stammered. "What?"

"I just had the urge to tell you that your grandfather's fine. I sensed you needed to know," I said, a little embarrassed.

"My grandfather died last week," he said.

"I know," I said, placing my hand on his arm, giving it a reassuring squeeze. "I need to tell you that Monday's going to be fine. And your grandparents are proud of you."

On hearing this news, the poor guy dropped his drink. All he could say was, "WOW!" He was completely gobsmacked. "Monday is his funeral. I have to write a speech and I don't know where to start."

"He's telling me to tell you to just say what comes naturally and not to worry so much."

My friend stood there smiling; she had seen me do this before. The guy, however, just stood there with a shocked look on his face. "I knew there was a reason I needed to come and talk to you two, but I didn't realize this was it. I thought I would just come to chat you girls up," he said finally.

I just smiled, and he looked at me and said, "Thank you, you really don't know how much this means to me."

I felt immense satisfaction in being able to help, but all I had done was repeat the words that were somehow given to me.

"Can I give you a hug?" he said, looking all sheepish. We hugged and I thought he would never let go of me, and then he walked away as if a heavy weight had been lifted off his shoulders. It made me feel all warm and fuzzy; I was energized. I never saw the guy again, but he seemed to have found peace and closure because of the little message I gave him.

As a result of those and other similar experiences, people who knew about my ability began to approach me, off-loading whatever was on their mind, thinking I'd be able to give them some insight or guidance. I did my best to help them, and even began to treat these occurrences as if they were normal, not "magical" or "strange." I was open to what I was seeing, feeling, and hearing, and if I sensed something that I thought might be of value to them, I was glad to share it, but it's not as if I was seeking it out on my own. Still, when I think back on it, I realize that I became more open to my abilities as a direct result of those people, probably because they believed in me long before I believed in myself.

In time, I became increasingly curious about my experiences, and I decided to seek out a few "real" psychics in order to try and get a better perspective. I'd heard about a popular woman in Welwyn Garden City, and having booked a mid-week appointment, made the short drive over on my day off.

I walked into the house and hadn't even sat down at her dining table when she smiled and said, "You're very gifted yourself."

"What do you mean *gifted*?"

"You can do this type of work, and you will do one day—you have the gift."

There was that word again: *gift*. I actually never interpreted these feelings and visions as being gifted; a musician is gifted, but not me.

There were nine packs of regular playing cards on the table in front of her, and she asked me to pick three. After shuffling them, she began telling me about the guy I'd just met, whom I quite liked, saying it wasn't going to work out, and of course I didn't like hearing

Photo by Colin Blake

Lisa and her beloved granddad

that. I had hoped that he and I were going to get serious. I hadn't allowed myself to become too intimately involved with any man since Paul had broken my heart, but I was hoping things would develop with this one. I wanted this psychic to tell me that he and I were the perfect match, and that true love was just around the corner. She moved on, still consulting the cards.

"Your grandfather will die with three people at his bedside."

"What does that mean?" I asked.

"I don't know."

"Am I one of the people?"

"No," she said.

I didn't want to believe that at all. . . . My granddad meant the world to me, and there was no way I wouldn't be at his side.

I don't recall any other details of the reading, but do remember leaving with very mixed emotions, not wanting to believe most of what she had told me.

A week later, however, my boyfriend became involved with someone else. The psychic had been right about him, so of course, I began to wonder if she was possibly right about everything else, including my gift.

I went to see other people—crystal ball readers, palm readers, mediums—but few of them impressed me. The fact is, I was making the mistake of looking to them for answers. I had grown bored with my job, I was tired of searching for Mr. Right, and I had become embroiled with a group of friends who, as a whole, were a negative influence.

In short, I was at a crossroads and quite a difficult one, and it was my most ardent hope that someone—anyone—would show me the way out.

One day I went to visit a psychic in Kensington Market, and I came away thinking she was the real deal. She said I wouldn't stay in my current job much longer, that I would do a lot of traveling in the not-too-distant future, and that my early successes would take place overseas. She also knew about a man I had just begun dating, even the type of work he did, but didn't much approve of him, and she said I should take a closer look at some of the other people with whom I was spending my free time. Most tellingly, she said I had a grandmother with the gift, whom she knew was ailing, and informed me that I would be following in her footsteps. I couldn't understand how she knew any of these things. It's very easy for a so-called psychic to give general information such as, "You are going to have some trouble with your back," because just about all of us, at some point in our lives, probably *will* have trouble with our backs, but she was both specific and accurate.

The psychic had asked for a personal item of mine to hold, and during the entire reading, she toyed with one of my rings, rubbing it between her fingers. After a pause, she went on to tell me that my mother was having heart problems, which I didn't know at the time, but which turned out to be true, and said I'd be having difficulties with my stomach, but that I'd come through it all right. She also said I'd earn some money as a singer, but that it wouldn't turn into a career. I remember having mixed emotions because she had told me things I had not been prepared for, and, many years later, that experience helped me become much more sensitive and more attuned to the feelings of my clients.

Not two weeks later, I drove home for a visit, and I went to see my grandmother straightaway. She was feeling poorly, and there was a note on her door—FRANCES ISN'T SEEING ANYONE TODAY. PLEASE CALL BACK ANOTHER DAY. I tapped on the window, three times in quick succession—a family code—and she came to the door and ushered me inside. As she led me to the lounge, I began to tell her all about the reading in London. She listened attentively, not interrupting, and when I was finally done she smiled at me and said, "I'm glad you mentioned that because there are a few things I need to tell you."

She stood up and had me follow her to the corner of the room, to the round table by the window where she read for her clients. I sat across from her and watched as she reached for her well-worn Tarot cards. She tapped her forefinger against the cards, and against the table, and said, "Lisa, I'm going to read for you now. But if I see my own death, I'm stopping."

Again, I had mixed emotions. I was extremely excited, but also a little nervous because the time had finally arrived. Nan had always said that she would never read for friends or family, and for some reason she was breaking a precedent. I was told to shuffle the cards and then put them into three piles representing past, present, and future. She then asked me to choose a pile to be discarded—this was the past.

"You can't change the past, so why look at it," she said.

Well, she was right about that!

She was only interested in discussing the present and the future. "The man you're seeing now," she began, "he's not the man for you. You will have many relationships, but you will only truly love twice. . . . You will have only one child, but I see the possibility of a connection to a second child." Then she looked up at me and said, "You will be famous."

"A record contract?" I said, excited. The more I sang at karaoke bars, the more I wanted to sing for a living.

"No," she said, and she smiled sweetly. "Not as a singer, Lisa. You're going to do what I do. You will follow in my footsteps. This is what you'll be known for."

"Really?" I said, remembering what other psychics had said.

"Yes, *really*," she said, smiling. "And you'll be famous in America."

"Hello! The woman in Kensington Market told me that too!"

Nan flipped another card, and one more after that. "I see two older men in your life," she went on. "One of them, you'll marry. The other, older than the first, will open a lot of doors for you and take you to America."

"That sounds exciting," I said, but I wasn't convinced. I honestly didn't think I had much talent for the type of work Frances did, and I still wasn't sure I was even that interested, but I didn't want to be dismissive. This was my grandmother, after all, and clearly she believed what she was telling me.

"Why are you looking at me like that?" she asked, amused by my confusion.

"I'm not sure," I said.

"You'll have to trust me," she said. "I have been waiting for the right time to read to you, and this was the right time. You needed to know this, Lisa."

"But I don't understand," I said. "If I'm supposed to be doing this type of work, how do I do it? Where do I begin?"

And she said, "Just trust your gut instinct. It will never let you down." She smiled and slowly got to her feet, indicating that the reading was over. She seemed to be studying a point in the air just behind me. "You have a purple and yellow light above your head," she said.

I turned my head and looked. "I can't see anything," I said.

"Of course you can't," she said, laughing. "But *I* can."

"Does it mean anything?"

"It most certainly does. It means you will go far in the spiritual realm, and that you will help countless people through your hard work and dedication."

I went home, not knowing what to think. My grandmother was a gifted medium, much in demand, and she'd shared her talents with people all over the world, so I had to believe there was an element of truth to what she'd told me. What's more, she was my grandmother, and I knew she wouldn't steer me wrong. Still, even if I did have the gift, how did one go about learning the correct way to use it?

When I returned to Stevenage, more curious than ever, I couldn't resist having a reading at least once a month. I went to many different readers, and every single one of them told me the exact same thing: *You should be doing this type of work.* Of course, as I suggested earlier, it's possible they could have said this very thing to everyone who came through their doors. After all, one's presence alone demonstrated an interest, and what could be more flattering than to be told that you had the gift, especially by someone who professed to know.

Even so, many of the readings were convincingly specific, and some of them confirmed many of the things I'd heard from my nan: I would live in America for a time. I would marry an older man. I would have only one son. The information was so eerily consistent that I decided I had to trust it, and I found myself becoming more deeply immersed in that whole world. I went and had my chart prepared by an astrologer. I bought a set of Tarot cards (though of course I had no idea what to do with them). And I read all sorts of books on the subject. My grandmother told me about someone whom she had met a few times: Doris Stokes, a British spiritualist who became quite well known in the 1980s. I discovered she had written several books, including *A Host of Voices*, in which she talks at length about communicating with the dead. She said she first became aware of her gift while still very young, when dead relatives began appearing before her, and of course this struck a chord with me. I discovered that she had been widely criticized by various Christian groups, along with the Church of England, for engaging in practices that were offensive to God, but I didn't see how they were offensive. She was giving comfort to people by helping them communicate with loved ones, and she was doing it successfully.

One day, as I was thinking about Doris, I was overcome with a feeling of *wholeness* and *connectedness*. It was the same feeling I'd experienced at thirteen, when—with the help of the Sunshine Group—I'd found God. I had been trying to figure out what to do with my life, beyond the gym, beyond the questionable friendships, beyond the unsatisfying, short-lived relationships, and suddenly I knew. I felt connected to something larger than myself, something that had been calling to me since I was three, when those ghostly faces began floating in and out of my bedroom walls. I can't tell you exactly *what* it was I felt connected to, or what had triggered it, but the feeling was real and unmistakable—and also very bizarre.

Feeling transformed by the experience, I decided it was time to make some drastic changes. I would leave my job and move away. After all, I had nothing to lose. I had no boyfriend, and I spent way too many nights in karaoke bars, nursing my ever-present Diet Coke in the company of people who were just as lost as I was. I was sick of it, frankly. The late nights. The endless conversations about nothing. The meaningless encounters. Every day I felt that I was traveling further on the wrong road and in the wrong direction.

My family knew nothing about this, of course. They thought my life was fabulous. I didn't want to let them know the real truth—the life I was ashamed of. I didn't want to disappoint them, so I put on a happy face. I thought leaving home was a way of changing my life for the good, and to a certain extent it was. Even so, at the time I felt more lost than ever. But on reflection, those times were so important because they molded me into the person I am today. I was growing up, not only mentally but spiritually.

As much as I longed for a change, I couldn't figure out where to start. A year went by, eighteen months, and I just couldn't get myself going. I was lethargic. I met a boy named Guy and thought he was the way out. I thought he was wonderful, but completely wrong for me, yet within weeks we were living together.

One Saturday morning in February, I woke up with an awful feeling in the pit of my stomach. It was early and I crept out of bed and started pacing the house. I couldn't work out why I was so irritable. I decided I needed to do something, so I did the washing and went outside to hang it. While I was outside I thought, *It's Nan. I'm going to get a call about Nan.* A moment later, Guy told me there was a phone call for me.

"It's my Dad, isn't it?"

He nodded. "How did you know?"

"It's about my grandmother, isn't it?"

He didn't say anything, but the look on his face told the story. He lowered his eyes as I ran to the house to pick up the phone.

"Dad?" I said.

"Lisa," he said, faltering. "Your nan's not doing too well. She's at Selly Oak Hospital. They are telling us that it's not looking good." You could hear the sadness in his voice.

"I'm on my way," I said.

In some ways, I think I had seen this coming. My grandmother had been in touch with two healers from spirit, both of them long dead, and a year earlier they had informed her that there was nothing more they could do to help her, and said they wouldn't be coming back.

Guy and I threw some clothes in a bag and started the long drive to Birmingham. I was just a kid the last time I went to Selly

Oak Hospital, but somehow we managed to find our way without a map, never stopping to ask directions and without a single wrong turn. It was as though someone was showing me the way and I was suddenly reminded of what Nan had told me: *Trust your gut instinct. It will never let you down.*

My family was there. My parents. My brother. Cousins, uncles. My grandmother had been unconscious most of the night, and everyone was bracing for the worst. I went up to the side of her bed and lifted her hand into both of mine. "Nan," I said. "I'm here."

Her eyes flickered open and she turned to look at me. Everyone reacted with surprise. I don't think they expected her ever to wake up again.

She kept staring straight at me, then squeezed my hand very tightly, and I rubbed her hand. She must have seen the tears in my eyes, but all I could think about was how frightened she looked. Then without warning, she closed her eyes again. I left the ward without saying anything to anyone, but inside I felt numb. I was so sad because I knew it was the end.

My cousin Tracey, who I hadn't seen for a long time, joined me in the cafeteria—we both needed a strong coffee. She started talking about how Nan had opened her eyes and maybe she would get through this. I just looked at her.

"It's over," I said. "She's not coming back."

"I don't believe that. She's been sick before. She'll pull through. She always does."

The following day, the nurses moved her into a quieter, less crowded ward. I asked one of the nurses if Nan was going to make it, and she looked at me solemnly. "It's rare for people to come back from this point," she said quietly. "I suggest you start saying your good-byes."

It was getting late and Tracey had gone home to take care of her children, but I thought she needed to be at the hospital. Around midnight, I drove out to her house to fetch her. By the time we returned, Nan had unfortunately taken another turn for the worse, and so, one by one, we went in to see her and say our private good-byes.

When it was my turn, I again held her hand in both of mine. "Remember that reading you gave me?" I began. "Well, if you're right about what you said, and I really am going to be doing this type of work in the years ahead, I can only hope I'm half as good as you." She was unconscious and didn't respond. I took a deep breath and went on. "Look, Nan, I know you're a little scared. Everyone is scared of the unknown. But you're already quite familiar with the spirit world, and in your heart you must know there's nothing to worry about. You've got plenty of friends and family on the other side waiting to greet you."

I felt her hand twitch, if only slightly, and I felt she had heard me. I leaned over and gave her a final kiss on the forehead, then turned and left the room. My parents were out in the corridor. "I have to go home," I told them and, having said my good-byes, walked away.

I drove the hundred miles back to Herfordshire, and went to bed exhausted.

I woke up with a start, thinking, *She's getting ready to let go.* I got dressed and had a light breakfast, and at nine o'clock on the nose—I remember looking at the clock—I was overcome by an urge to call the hospital. There was no answer at the ward. I was agitated and after trying a third time, I knew in my heart that it was over. I called the house a few hours later and my aunt Linda answered. I said, "Hey, it's me, Lisa. I've been trying all morning to find out some news. I couldn't get through at the hospital."

"Your nan died this morning," she said.

"When?" I asked, but I already knew the answer.

"At nine o'clock."

When I got off the phone, I felt totally empty. This was the first family death I really had to deal with. I sat in the chair, unable to move, but I began to review my life (as you do on such occasions). I decided that I needed to change. It wouldn't be like last time, either. This time I would *really change*. I wasn't getting much joy out of anything. Not my work, not my friends, not anything! My grandmother's death seemed like a signal of some sort. It would inspire me to make a new start.

But again I couldn't get motivated. The days turned into weeks, the weeks into months, and I was stuck in a rut, unable to break out. I continued to live the life I was living, partying, burning the candle at both ends, smiling and pretending to be having a good time. I'd get home exhausted every night, sometimes as late as 4 a.m., and collapse on the bed, promising to change. *I'll start tomorrow*, I told myself. But tomorrow never came.

I'd been living in Arlesley with Guy in a two-bedroom maison-nette, a small, self-contained apartment with a lovely, pastel-yellow bedroom that I'd decorated on my own. I'm not much for interior design, but I poured a lot of energy into that room—probably to avoid thinking about my dead-end life—and I really loved the way it turned out. One night, I was in the bedroom, putting away the laundry. My two cats, Tiger and Chloe, were watching me from their perch at the end of the bed, when suddenly Chloe hissed and shot off the bed and ran straight out of the room. I watched her tail disappear through the door and into the corridor, and when I turned back I saw Tiger's hair standing on end. A moment later he shot out of the room, too. I was wondering what had spooked them, when suddenly I saw my grandmother sitting on the edge of the bed, large as life. Not surprisingly, I panicked; I didn't know what to do or say. Time seemed to stand still. Sure, I'd seen dead people before but this seemed more *real*. Looking back I regret what happened next and I would do anything to have that moment again, but I took a deep breath, trying to calm myself. "Nan," I said. "I can't deal with this. Please go away."

She looked up at me and smiled, and it occurred to me that this was an earlier version of my grandmother—a woman I'd known long ago, vibrant and jolly and happy—but her presence still scared the hell out of me. "It's your turn now," she said tenderly.

I grabbed my car keys and literally ran out of the house, not even closing the door behind me, and I jumped into my car and sped off. I didn't know where I was going, and I didn't much care, but I knew I had to get out. I couldn't quite wrap my head around what had just happened. I drove around aimlessly, and as I began to calm down I remember feeling guilty about having run out on her. "Nan," I said. "If you're listening, I'm sorry. I just freaked out when I saw you."

I eventually turned the car around and drove home. The front door was still open. I went inside and crept upstairs, still worrying that Nan would be waiting on the bed, perhaps a little cross with me. She wasn't there, of course, and I felt simultaneously relieved and disappointed. I was relieved because I didn't have to deal with her, but disappointed because there was so much I wanted to talk to her about. I wanted to tell her that I felt lost and directionless and totally confused, and that I kept trying to change my life without success. And that's when it occurred to me: I wasn't really trying. I was telling myself I'd try, but I was doing nothing to effect real change. And that's when everything changed for me.

I finally acknowledged my situation and the negativity surrounding it. I knew what I had to do, and I somehow knew that I would be given help and support in ways I had never experienced before my nan passed. I quit my job without having another lined up, but two weeks later, I was offered a new position at a gym in Biggleswade, in Bedfordshire. I called my friends, one at a time, to say good-bye. It was the hardest decision I had had to make at that time. As individuals, I valued each of them, but I could no longer live the life that they led. There were a few who didn't respect my decision and the only thing I could do was ignore their calls. I didn't have the willpower to resist their unhealthy influences, and the only way to break free was to put some real distance between us.

Finally, I walked away from *that* life!

I adapted to the new job quickly enough. I loved the gym atmosphere, everyone was so lovely, but I found it uninspiring, and I hungered for real change. One day I saw an ad in the paper for a Butlins Redcoat. Butlins are these good old-fashioned British holiday camps, and the Redcoats provide the entertainment. They sing and dance and entertain the guests, and it sounded a good deal more lively than working in a gym, especially since this was based in a hotel in the center of London.

I sent in an application, describing myself as fun-loving and bubbly, with a little experience as a singer, and I was called in for an audition. I sang "Flashdance . . . What a Feeling" and my grand-dad's favorite song, "Wind Beneath My Wings." It was amazing being on stage. I loved it, but after watching the other auditions—some of which were really superb—I didn't think I'd get the job. A week went by. When I hadn't heard anything, I gave up hope and started to consider other options. Then out of the blue, I had a call from the entertainment manager, who told me I got the job. I was so happy I screamed into the phone!

"Lisa," she said, laughing. "Are you all right?"

"Oh my God. Yes!" I said.

"Do you still want the job?" she asked.

"What! Are you kidding? Of course I do!"

This was exactly the change I needed. So that was it. . . . I gave up my boyfriend and my cats and went to work at the Butlins Hotel in Bayswater, in West London. Right from the start, it was like having an instant, close-knit family. There were twelve of us Redcoats, and we lived together in the basement of the hotel. We ate together, played together, and partied together at the end of the day. But we worked, too, of course—very hard. We put on shows, entertained the guests, took large groups to restaurants in and around London, and even gave sightseeing tours aboard double-decker buses. It was a lot like being a camp counselor, but for adults and it was one of the best jobs I had ever had—I had so much fun!

I celebrated my twenty-fourth birthday with my new family—the year was 1997—and I couldn't have been happier. But not long after I'd arrived, it started again. I would sense things. Hear things. See things. On the third floor of the hotel, for example, just beyond the elevator banks, I used to see a little boy walking up and down the long, dark corridor, crying. He was maybe four or five years old, with dark hair, and he would pace back and forth like a tiny prisoner, dragging his blanket. I felt bad for him, but I didn't try to talk to him. I don't know why, exactly. Maybe I thought I'd feel worse if I knew what he was crying about.

I also ran into an angry old woman in the basement laundry, where the hotel linens were stored. She had gray hair, tied back in a bun, and she never spoke, but for some reason I sensed that she was foreign. She would walk past, muttering under her breath, and she'd always slam the door on her way out. The door didn't actually close, although some people thought they heard it slamming, but I could *see* it, which made the whole experience even more off-putting.

One morning, a few of us had a day off, so we decided that we should visit the London Dungeons. We were all very excited, but when we got there I found I couldn't go inside. I was totally overwhelmed by the negative energy, and I could hear muted screams coming from below. I never went in. I could sense evil all around me, and it was so palpable that I knew it was real, and it scared me.

On more than one occasion, back at the hotel, a woman's voice would wake me in the middle of the night, calling out urgently: "Lisa! Lisa!" There was no one there, however, and I never heard more than my name.

Throughout this period, I felt that I was evolving, which confused me, since I had done nothing to consciously develop this talent—and, in fact, despite my previous convictions, had been trying to ignore it. But London was awash in history, and it seemed as if the past was calling out to me. And it wasn't just the spirit world, either. I remember a colleague coming back from a weekend with his girlfriend, talking very convincingly about what a wonderful time they'd had. I could tell things had gone badly, however. "Tell me how it *really* went," I said.

"How did you know we had problems?" he asked.

I still didn't understand where this stuff came from. "I just knew," I said. "But you're going to hear from her, and everything's going to be all right."

That very instant, his mobile rang. He fished it out of his pocket and looked at it, then turned to me, astonished. "It's her," he said.

"I know," I said, secretly pleased with myself.

Another colleague, a girl, had a mad crush on one of the other Redcoats, and I took her aside one day and said, "I know you like David, but I have to tell you it's not going to happen."

She looked at me as I was off my trolley. "How did you know about David?" she said in a furtive whisper, pulling me off to one side. "I haven't said a word about it. *He* doesn't even know."

"I just get a feeling," I said.

"Feeling?"

"It's hard to explain. It's like I know stuff. Sounds sort of witchy I know, but it's really not and I'm never wrong."

She studied me for a moment, confused, and suddenly looked hopeful. "Can you tell how it's going to turn out?"

"It's not," I said, and I tried to be as gentle as possible. "He's seeing someone else but hasn't told anyone."

"How do you know? Has he told you?"

"No, I just have a feeling." And sure enough, once again, I was right.

In very short order, as a result of other, similar experiences, word got out: *Lisa is a bit weird; Lisa sees things and has feelings.* But I didn't fight it anymore. Some people, nonbelievers, simply dismissed me, but many others were intrigued, and they would seek me out for guidance and advice. I never gave actual readings. I just told them what I thought of situations they were in. Still, it was a strange position to find myself in, and it reminded me of what my grandmother had told me: "Lisa, it's your turn now."

It seemed that she might be right.

That same week, while I was flipping though a magazine, a little voice in my head told me that I was overdue for a medical checkup. I called the National Health Service (NHS) to schedule an appointment, and the following week I had a complete checkup, including a Pap smear. The doctor was only a few minutes into the exam when she stopped what she was doing and looked up at me. "How long has it been since your last checkup?" she asked.

"About five years, I'd think."

"Why did you wait so long?"

"My last doctor told me the smear was good for ten years," I said.

She looked completely amazed. "It's only good for three years," she said.

"Is something wrong?" I asked.

Without elaborating, she said, "I'm going to refer you to the hospital."

I went back to the hotel and tried not to think about it. After all, the NHS doesn't move very fast; normally I would have to wait three months for an appointment. But a week later a letter arrived asking me to report to St. Mary's Hospital, in Paddington, that very Friday. I didn't really worry about it, though. I thought perhaps the bureaucracy had improved by leaps and bounds, and that this really had nothing to do with my individual case.

On Friday, I went in, as scheduled, for a colposcopy, which is what's called for if the Pap smear appears abnormal. The doctor kept looking at the monitor, which showed my procedure, and I could see what she was looking at—but of course I didn't have a clue whether the news was good or bad. Then I noticed the look on her face and I began to worry a little. "Is something wrong?" I asked.

"I'm not sure," she said. "I don't want you to worry. I'll call you as soon as the results are back."

She called three days later. I was in my room at Butlins, on my bed, learning a song I was scheduled to perform that night. We exchanged friendly hellos, and she plunged right in: "If we had caught this earlier, these cells would have been precancerous, but unfortunately we didn't catch them in time."

"What are you saying? I have cancer?" I said, shocked. I don't know how I managed to get the words out. I was in total disbelief.

"Now, don't get scared," she said. "It's going to be okay. But I'd like you to come and see me as soon as you can."

I didn't answer. Her words were a complete wash. None of it was sinking in.

"Lisa, are you there?"

"Yes."

"I'd like you to come and see me as soon as you can," she repeated. "Tomorrow would be good."

"I'll get back to you," I said, and I hung up.

At that point I went into complete denial. I carried on with the new song, went off to have dinner with my colleagues, performed and danced with the guests, and finished my shift at 1 a.m. as if it was a normal night for me. I don't remember even thinking about what the doctor had told me.

The next day, I did my job, as usual. I took a group on the bus sightseeing tour, and in the evening I took another group to dinner and a show.

For days on end, the doctor kept calling—the name of the hospital clearly visible in my mobile's screen—and for days on end I refused to answer. A week into it, while I was in the shower, my friend reached for my ringing mobile. When I got back to the room, she gave me a stern look and said, "Your doctor called. She wants you to call her back right away."

"Okay," I said.

"Lisa, she said she's been calling you for a week, and she said it's urgent. I really think you need to call her back now."

This is what finally shook me out of it. I know it had been crazy to ignore the doctor, but I wanted so much not to have cancer that I thought I could make it go away by pretending she didn't exist. It had worked with the faces in the bedroom. Why not with this?

The next day, at the end of my shift, I went to the hospital. I hadn't even bothered making an appointment—my mind still wasn't working right—and the receptionist looked up at me with surprise.

"I'm here to see the doctor," I said.

"Do you have an appointment?"

"No, I don't, but she's been calling me for a few days. My name is Lisa Williams."

"She's with patients, but I know she wants to see you, so please take a seat," she said with great politeness.

A short time later, I found myself in the examining room, facing the unavoidable truth. I had cervical cancer. The doctor kept handing me leaflets and pamphlets—Cancer Awareness, Cervical Cancer FAQs, etc.—and talking about what she intended to do for me. I barely heard half of it. "It's not that serious," she said, smiling. I kept thinking, *That's easy for you to say; you're not the one who has to deal with this!*

"We'll do some laser surgery, scoop the cancer cells away, and you'll be fine."

A few long days later—this was in late July—I had the procedure. I was scared and nervous but was in and out of the hospital before I knew it, and the doctor sent me away with a big pot of pills and directions on when and how to take them. I didn't even think to ask what I was taking. I believe the whole experience had left me in mild shock. I still could not accept that I had had cancer at such a young age.

I took three days off from work, which I had coming, anyway, and when I went back to work nobody had a clue about what I'd just been through. I felt physically horrible, but I carried on as best I could. I was determined to make a success of this job.

The following Sunday we took a group of the hotel guests to the Beefeater, which has a medieval motif and a show where Henry VIII walks between the guests with one of his many wives. There was lots of singing and dancing, with loads of food, but my fellow Redcoats and I had seen the show so many times, we didn't enjoy the experience.

Once the guests were settled, I went outside and called my mom. We made small talk for a few minutes, and then I told her—without drama, without fanfare—about the cancer. I could hear her beginning to panic on the phone. "Do you want me to come and get you?" she asked.

"No, I'm fine. They got it all."

"Are you sure?"

"Positive," I said.

I know it sounds odd, but that's just the type of person I am. I've never been a big complainer or one to get overemotional. As my father had foretold, life's lessons have toughened me up.

Even so, I felt bad about keeping the extent of my illness from my family. It would have been nice to go home, crawl into bed for a few days, and have Mom take care of me. But I couldn't do it. I knew I'd get through this on my own. I was twenty-four years old and despite the fact that my life wasn't perfect, I told myself that one day I would be on top of the world.

*Lisa performing one of the many
shows at Butlins (fourth from left)*

chapter 3

Men

About five weeks after the surgery, I finally began to feel a little better. I had run through my regimen of pills, and I never thought to connect the pills to the nausea and the rest of the horrid feelings I experienced, but there you have it—that business about the cure being worse than the disease. Interestingly enough, as my health improved I became increasingly unhappy with my work and some of the people I worked with. I enjoyed entertaining guests, and I really loved to sing, but life felt suddenly more fragile, and I decided it was time to move on again. *Really* move on this time. It also occurred to me that it's hard to move on when you're too comfortable, so not one to make it easy for myself, I gave notice before I'd found another job. I wanted desperately to stay in London and, fortunately, one of my friends had a small flat in town. He offered to let me stay there until I was on my feet and even said he'd be glad to pick me up in front of the hotel on the Saturday morning after my final day at work.

I worked until 1:00 a.m. on Friday, slept a few hours, and at 8:00 a.m. I bid a sad goodbye to my colleagues, packed my bags, and went out front to wait for my friend. I called him a few times and left messages, but by twelve o'clock I finally realized he wasn't coming. I somehow knew I couldn't rely on him, but I wanted to believe it would happen. As my Nan always advised, I should have listened to my feelings and saved myself the heartache.

I picked up my bags and made my way to the tourist hostel across the street. I was down to my last two hundred pounds, and the best they could offer me was a share in a room for ninety pounds a week. I took it. There were five other girls in my room, mostly foreigners; I could have offered to show them the sights of London, but instead I spent the whole weekend writing in my journal and trying to plan the rest of my life.

On Monday, I managed to get a job selling advertising space for a magazine. It consisted of making cold calls eight hours a day, five days a week. I hated it. People would tell me in no uncertain terms that they didn't want any bleeding advertising in any of our bleeding magazines, and I would thank them politely and move on to the next name on the list. It was one of the hardest jobs I'd ever had, and it only paid 115 pounds a week. Ninety of that went toward my share at the hostel, where I had a constant rotation of new roommates, and I spent fifteen on a seven-day tube pass in order to get to and from work. That left me only ten pounds a week, so I learned to live on flapjacks alone. It was unhealthy and exhausting, and on weekends I hardly ever left my room; I spent the time reading or writing in my journal.

"Things are wonderful!" I told my mom. "The job's not great, but I sold a few spots this past week, so I'm not complaining. I'm really enjoying London. It's fabulous!"

At one point, I was so desperate that I thought about getting in touch with my old friends who I had left behind. I knew I would be welcomed back with open arms and it would be as if nothing had changed. I picked up the phone a few times only to put it down when someone answered. I just couldn't do it. I couldn't go back. I was worth so much more than that!

I was struggling. I was hungry. And more than once the thought crossed my mind to look through the trash for food. I only had a bottle of water a day and the rest of the time I drank from the taps in the bathroom. I was desperate now, but I still didn't want to admit to it. I remember when it was my time of the month, and I needed to get some supplies for which I had no money. I didn't want to do it but I had no choice: "Mom, is there any chance you can put ten pounds in my bank account? I've just got my period and I'm a little tight on money and I need to get some tampons."

I could just imagine what was going through my mom's head. Finally she said, "Why didn't you tell me that it had gotten this bad?"

I couldn't say anything in response. I just cried.

"I'm coming to get you," she said.

"Okay" was all I could sputter. The reality was I wanted my mom to look after me and protect me. Three hours later, she and Dad arrived in London and took me home. I spent a week there, eating well, being well loved, visiting with my nan and my grand-dad, and recuperating. I also went to visit my old friend Sarah, who worked in a salon in Stratford-on-Avon, and who insisted on doing my hair. "Life has not turned out exactly as planned," I told her. "Then again, I'm not sure I planned anything exactly."

When eventually I went back to London, I had renewed spirit and things finally began falling into place. I found a fabulous room in Paddington with two Nigerian brothers, the two sweetest, most respectful guys I'd ever met, and I landed a job as a barmaid at The Globe, a very popular bar in Moorgate. I worked Monday to Friday and loved every minute of it. I spent the weekend exercising, taking long walks, and going on an occasional date.

After three months, I was feeling more clearheaded than I had in a long time. I decided I wanted to go back to university to become a qualified physical education teacher. Despite my mediocre grades, I was now considered a "mature student," and I was accepted to De Montfort University, back in Bedfordshire. I left London and moved into a flat with an old friend. I loved being in university—I practiced dance, gymnastics, and swimming, and I had never enjoyed myself so much. I was one of the oldest in the course and was known affectionately as "Granny." I hung around with a great guy called James who was also a mature student, and he became known as "Granddad."

To cover my tuition and living expenses, I took a part-time job selling time-shares for vacation rentals, and within a few months I was promoted to manager at the company's local office. I ended up falling for one of the regional sales managers, Reg. He was twenty years older than I, and very bright and witty with the bluest eyes you ever saw. One afternoon, after weeks of small talk, he suddenly asked me out. "I'm on the road six days out of seven," he said, "but next time I'm in Bedfordshire I'd love to have dinner with you."

"All right, yes," I said, a bit startled. "That would be nice."

We went out, and then we went out again, and when he was out of town, which was often, we talked on the phone every night for at least two hours. I found myself opening up to him like I'd never opened up to anyone in my life. I felt more connected to him than I'd ever felt to anyone, and I didn't even have to think about it when he eventually asked me to marry him.

I ended up moving to his place in Lancashire, taking a position at a branch office there, and managed to transfer to a local university to continue my studies. The day after I arrived, Reg introduced me to his mother, and the first thing she said to me was, "You have a psychic awareness, don't you?"

I told her about my grandmother, and about some of my experiences with the spirit world, and she went into another room and came back with a deck of Tarot cards. "I dabble in this stuff myself, so I knew you had the gift the moment my son brought you through that door. Will you read for me sometime?"

"I couldn't, really," I said. "I don't know the first thing about this."

"But you do," she said. "I insist."

I wasn't so sure. I spent time trying to study the Tarot cards, but they just didn't make sense. I had no idea how to interpret them. But that little voice in my head said, "Forget the meaning of the cards, just go with your gut feelings."

Finally, I plucked up enough courage to do a reading. Reg was away on business, but I invited his mother around. We sat on my bed across from each other and I asked her to shuffle the deck, remembering how my grandmother had done it, then asked her to split the cards into three piles.

"One for the past, one for the present, and one for the future," I said. I felt I was being guided along by Nan. "My grandmother used to say you can't change the past, so we won't bother with the first pile."

I asked her to choose one of the remaining piles, and I began to flip through the cards. "A gentleman will enter your life, but you will never marry again," I began. I didn't even sound like myself. *A gentleman will enter your life?* Where had that come from? I talked to her about her health, about her finances, about her interest in Reiki, a Japanese healing art, and when we were done, she seemed quite impressed. "You're really very good at this, you know. You shouldn't let a gift of that magnitude go to waste."

When she left, I wondered whether she was simply being nice, given my relationship with her son, or whether it was time to get serious about this whole business. But I continued to do nothing. I was enjoying work, and I was keeping my head afloat in school, so in a sense I was again too comfortable to try to effect any change.

The only negative in my life was the fact that Reg was always travel-ing, and I didn't have any control over that. Still, it wasn't easy. This was the man I was going to marry, but I felt more single and more alone than I'd ever felt in my life.

One day I went to lunch with Caroline, one of the girls from the office, and she confided that she had been working as a medium. When I told her about my grandmother, and my own limited experiences in that world, she said, "I knew there was something about you. That's why I asked you to lunch—to share this with you. Nobody at the office knows I do readings. I'm sure most of them would think me daft."

"You mean you think I have the gift?" I said.

"I know you have the gift," she said. "If you want me to help you with it, I will."

I thought for a while and finally asked, "When can we start?"

"As soon as you like," she said.

In the days and weeks ahead, with Reg out of town so often, Caroline and I spent a great deal of time together. "When I'm with a client, and an image comes to me, I study it closely for clues," Caroline said. "What time of year is it? Where is the person stand-ing? Is there anything around the spirit that will help me or my client decipher what I'm seeing? Is he or she wearing short sleeves? Is the weather hot? Are the surroundings nice or shabby? Are we indoors or out? Do I hear anything—the wind, the ocean, other voices?"

One Friday after work, we went out for a drink, and Caroline had one too many. "I don't trust myself to drive home," she said.

"You can stay at my place," I said.

"Won't Reg mind?"

"Reg is working," I said. "Reg is *always* working."

When we got back to the house, Caroline wasn't ready for bed. She dropped onto the couch and said, "Let's see if you can pick anything up about me; just tell me what you see."

"It's odd you said that," I remarked. "Because there's a gentleman standing directly across the room." I pointed at a smartly dressed gentleman, but she couldn't see him. "He's sort of like a father figure to you, but he's not your father," I said. "I sense he died of a heart attack."

When I turned to look at Caroline, her eyes had welled up with tears. "That's my adopted dad," she said. "He died of a heart attack last year."

The experience was quite intense for Caroline, but it was equally intense for me. I had never done anything like that in my life. I was sitting in my living room with a friend from work, and I had just acknowledged that I could see her relative who had passed over.

"Is he still there?" she asked.

I looked back to find him gone. "No," I said, a little disappointed.

"I never spoke about this at work, so you couldn't have found this out from anyone we know," she said.

I told Caroline that I had some Tarot cards but had no idea what I was supposed to do with them. She suggested I buy some Psycards, which are similar to Tarot cards, but simpler and easier to decipher. I bought a set the next morning and went home and started playing with them, just shuffling them about and trying to get some feelings, and within minutes the spirit of a little blond girl ran across the room. She was smiling and happy, and for some reason I knew her name was Abigail—it just popped into my head—but I knew absolutely nothing else about her. (I only recently discovered that she was the daughter of my friend, Ian, and had died around the same time as I had seen her.)

The next day, Reg called to say he wouldn't be home that weekend, and I couldn't help but whine a bit. "You're never home," I said. "I never see you."

"You'll see plenty of me when we're married," he said.

Later that night, exhausted and full of self-pity, I called my friend Sarah, the hairdresser in Stratford-on-Avon, and we got to complaining about our respective men. When I was done lambasting Reg for his extended absences, she began to talk about her boyfriend, Tony. But I cut her off in mid-sentence. "He's cheating on you," I said.

"What?"

"Tony. He's cheating on you."

"What are you talking about?"

"I'm not sure. You know how I get these thoughts and feelings. Well I'm getting one now, and it's very strong." It *was* very strong. It was also true that I didn't know exactly what I was talking about. It felt as if the words had spilled from my mouth of their own volition.

"Who's he cheating with, then?"

"Someone called Lisa," I said. "Not me!" I added quickly. "It's another Lisa. He met her in a bar. The Red Lion; The Red Bird; something with 'red' in it. And she's been around for two."

"Two what?"

"I don't know. I just see the number two. I'm not sure what it means."

"This is crazy," she said.

"I'm sorry," I said. I felt a bit light-headed, as if I was coming out of a trance.

"What else do you see?"

"Nothing."

"Can't you try a little harder?"

"Whatever it was, it's gone," I said. "I don't want you to feel badly about this. It was just a feeling. I have no idea where it came from. And it's probably wrong."

I fell asleep immediately after we got off the phone.

A few days later, Sarah called. I had barely managed a hello when she blurted out: "Lisa is a barmaid at The Red Lion."

"What?"

"Lisa, don't you remember? You told me Tony was seeing someone, and you saw something with the word 'red' in the name."

The memory came back to me, but only vaguely. I remember going to bed right after we spoke, and collapsing in exhaustion.

"The night you told me about it, they'd already been seeing each other for two weeks," Sarah said.

"Two weeks?"

"Don't you remember? You saw the number two, but you didn't know what it meant."

"Of course," I said.

"You were spot on!"

"Does he know you know?"

"He does now," she said. "And I'm done with him. I'm done with men full stop!"

After we got off the phone, I felt sorry for her. Here she was, alone again, and I was getting married in three months. On May 9, 1999, to be precise. The date had a nice ring to it. But as the day got closer, I began to have serious misgivings about Reg. Why was I marrying the guy? He was never there. I didn't even know him. But I did nothing. I was paralyzed by fear and indecision as the date crept ever closer.

In late March, three weeks before the wedding—and mind, I don't believe in coincidences—I got a letter from the hospital. I'd been having regular Pap smears since the cancer scare a year earlier, and everything seemed normal, but suddenly my London doctor wanted to see me. I called Reg and told him I would like him to go with me.

"What's it about?" he asked.

"I'm not sure. But I'm nervous."

"Well, I'm in Dublin until late Sunday," he said.

"That's fine," I said. "The appointment's at ten-thirty Monday morning. It'll work perfectly. You can either fly into London from Dublin or you can drive down and meet me."

It was a four-hour drive from Lancashire to London. I'd told him I'd drive to my parents in Birmingham the night before, which was about halfway there, and pick him up at Heathrow early Monday morning.

"Then I'd be without a car, wouldn't I?" he said.

"Isn't this more important?" I asked.

Apparently, it wasn't. No matter what I suggested, he came up with a reason why it wouldn't work. "Fine," I said, angry by now. "I do everything else on my own, so I guess I can manage this."

On Saturday, I went to my parents' house, and I didn't mention anything about Reg or about the doctor. Mom was excited about the wedding, which she had been helping me plan, but she wanted to know that everything was going to work out. "Lisa," she said brightly. "Will you read for me?"

This surprised me because I'd never read for my mother before, and Frances had steadfastly refused to read for any members of the family—at least until the fateful day she read for me—but I didn't see the harm in it, so I went out to the car to get my cards.

She sat on the sofa and I sat on the floor in front of her, and the first thing I saw hit me like a bombshell: There would be no wedding. "It's going to be a lovely wedding," I lied and avoided making eye contact with her. "Everything's going to go as planned."

"In that case, let's go and get my wedding outfit!" Mom said.

I already had my wedding dress—I'd gone into Stevenage a month earlier, with Mom and Nan, and fallen in love with a quietly elegant white dress—but Mom still hadn't found anything to wear, and she desperately needed a hat: The mother of the bride *must* have a hat.

We went into town and found a lovely hat for three hundred pounds. It was expensive, but she looked stunning in it, and when we got home she couldn't stop trying it on. "It is lovely, isn't it?" she said.

"For three hundred pounds, it better be lovely," I said.

I felt awful. Not only had I lied to my mother, I had just blown three hundred hard-earned pounds on her hat.

On Monday, I drove to Paddington, in London, to sit with my

doctor. "Well, it's been a year now, and I'm glad to see you haven't had a problem," she said. "Your Pap smears are still abnormal, but it's nothing to worry about. Still, it pays to be cautious, so I'm going to transfer your file to a colleague in Lancashire, and I want you to promise to see her every three months."

"I will," I said. She was lovely, but I sensed that she had more to tell me. "Was there something else?" I asked.

"Well, yes," she said, hesitating. "I'm sorry to say this, but I think it's highly unlikely you'll have children."

"I sort of knew that," I said. And I did. I think she'd more or less hinted at the possibility during the procedure, and in my heart I had begun to accept it, so I wasn't completely overwhelmed by the news, as devastating as it is for a woman to hear.

When I left the hospital, I wandered around London for a bit, and I stopped in at a bar for what they call a ploughman's lunch: cheddar cheese, a roll, a pickle, and a small salad. As I ate, I wondered how Reg would feel about not having children. We had spoken about kids, albeit briefly, and I knew he wanted them.

After lunch, still lost in thought, I kept wandering around London. I walked through Trafalgar Square to the Embankment, on the River Thames, and stood staring at the Oxo Building across the way. It's beautiful when it's lit up at night, with London Bridge and Tower Bridge visible in the distance. I watched a double-decker bus humming past, filled with tourists. I remembered my time at Butlins, smiling, and had to fight the urge to break into song.

Finally, I got on the tube and returned to where I'd parked my car, near the hospital, and made the long drive back to Lancashire. It was during that drive that I decided I couldn't marry Reg. I didn't really know him all that well, I realized, but his refusal to accompany me to London, when I genuinely needed him, told me everything I needed to know. I deserved better. I was as insecure as the next twenty-five-year-old, maybe more so, but was I so insecure that I was willing to marry a man that I didn't love? What was wrong with me? I'd always stood on my own two feet. Reg had many good qualities—he was worldly, he was smart, and he was loving when he wanted to be—but he came up short where it mattered. From the start, our relationship had been about Reg. What he wanted. What he needed. *When* he wanted and needed it. But what about me? The one time I'd asked him to be there for me, the one time I'd allowed myself to show some vulnerability, Reg had been more concerned about being trapped in London without his car. I couldn't be with someone with priorities like that. I couldn't see marrying him, and I certainly couldn't see myself with him in forty years. I had to be true to myself, for both our sakes.

On the drive home, I took a detour to Morecambe Bay to look at the waves and to think about what I was on the verge of doing. I arrived at the house shortly after 8:30 that night. Reg was home, waiting for me, standing in the kitchen in his flip-flops and jeans, with his ever-present cigar, and he gave me a little kiss.

"How'd it go at the doctor's?" he asked.

"Fine," I said. "Everything's fine."

"You see? I knew it was nothing."

I looked at him for a long time, wondering how to break the news.

"What?" he said, staring back at me, and pausing to flick an ash into the sink.

"Reg," I said. "I don't think I'm ready to get married."

He started to pace up and down, clearly agitated, then stubbed out his cigar and turned to face me. "What about all the people who are coming to the wedding?" he said.

"Well, we're giving them two weeks notice. I'm sure they'll understand."

"What about all the money I've spent?"

"I'm sure we can get some of it back."

"No, we can't! Half the stuff is nonrefundable."

"Is that what this is about to you?" I said. "The money? You don't marry someone just because you've spent some money."

"It's my money!" he shouted.

"I know that," I said. "And I'm sorry. But there are bigger issues here. I really needed you to come to London with me. I was nervous about the doctor, worried it would be bad news. Was it too much to ask to have you by my side?"

"I was in Dublin," he said.

I was crushed. That was his answer? *I was in Dublin.* "I'm exhausted," I said. "I'm going to bed."

In the morning, I left for work before Reg was up. He'd been traveling for six straight days, and he had the day off. I called him from the office a little later, feeling bad about the previous night, but my resolve didn't weaken. I reiterated what I'd told him: The marriage was off. He was actually very sweet about it. He didn't apologize for not having gone to the doctor with me, but he said he understood why I was upset, and that was *almost* as good.

I drove home after work, and just before I stepped through the door I had an eerie feeling that I was about to walk into a war zone. Reg was in the kitchen, smoking a cigar, and we exchanged quiet hellos, then I went upstairs to change and wash my face. As soon as I walked into the bathroom, I noticed that my things were gone. I went and looked in the closet, and all my clothes were gone too. I went back downstairs and asked him, as calmly as possible, where my stuff was.

"If you don't want to marry me," he said, "it's obviously because you're having an affair."

"An affair? That's crazy! I'm not having an affair!"

"I want you out of my life," he said. It was really nasty, the way he said it, and it scared me.

"Okay," I said. "Where's my stuff? I paid for that stuff. It's all I own in the world."

I noticed that even the pictures of us were gone. It was as if he had spent the entire day trying to wipe away every last trace of me.

"I want you out of here *now*," he said. "I know you're having an affair."

"But I'm not!" I repeated. "Where on earth did you get such an idea?"

Things went from bad to worse. I went through the house trying to find anything that belonged me to me, but it was all gone. "Why are you doing this?" I said, and I could feel the blood rushing to my head and a dryness in my throat.

"Go back to the gutter where you started," he said. "Go back to the life you deserve."

I was shocked. I had never seen this side of him, and it frightened me. I could talk to the dead, and I could see things that hadn't even happened yet, but I'd been completely blind to the flesh-and-blood man who stood before me.

"I must have been crazy," he said. "I can't imagine what possessed me to propose to you."

I left the house with nothing—I had no money, nothing except for my phone—and I called home. "Hi, Mom," I said.

"Hello, Lis. Are you okay?"

"No, I'm coming home," I said, crying.

There was a pause on her end. She knew I was in a bad way.

"Mom," I said, and I began to sob. "I can't go through with it."

"Just come home," she said, in a sweet, calming voice. "You know there's always a bed here for you."

I drove home, sobbing my heart out, and the next day my sorrow gave way to anger. I was furious with Reg. I couldn't believe he would treat me like that.

Mom made me feel safe and forced me to eat a little something, and Dad walked around in a state of shock. "I don't understand it," he said. "Is there anything I can do?" He'd always been a problem-solver, my dad, and he thought he could find a solution now. "It's okay," I said. "I'm all right. I guess it wasn't meant to be."

So there I was, nearly twenty-five years old, a week and a half away from a wedding that wasn't going to happen, once again living with my mom and dad in Redditch, taking stock of my so-called life. What had it all amounted to? Nothing much, I guess, since I was being forced to start my life all over again.

By week's end, still hurting but somewhat recovered, I went to an employment agency and got a job in the sales office at Linread Northbridge, a company that manufactures aeronautical parts. I didn't care what the job entailed. I just wanted a fresh start. On Saturday, I got a call from my friend Sarah. She was organizing a big karaoke party and absolutely insisted that I help her out. "We're going to get your mojo back," she said. "Just come along and you'll have a great time."

"Yeah, yeah," I said, unconvincingly.

"Oh, shut up! Enough of this feeling sorry for yourself," she said.

I got off the phone and told Mom I was going out. "I have a feeling that tonight I am going to meet someone who is going to change my life forever."

Not surprisingly, she looked at me dismissively. And I can't say I blamed her: The last time we'd talked about these types of feelings, I'd assured her that my wedding was going to be a lovely affair.

That night, I got myself together, slipped into my leopard-skin print jeans—very helpful in the old days, when I wanted to pull in a man—and told myself that I was going to have a good time.

The party was in a big barn. There were bars set up at both ends, and just out back they were roasting an entire pig. The stage was at one end of the room, and it wasn't long before I found myself up there, belting out the Celine Dion hit "My Heart Will Go On." I noticed a man watching me from near the entrance, apparently mesmerized, and when I was done he sought me out and smiled brightly. "You've got a big voice, haven't you?" he said. He was tall, with blond hair and a prominent nose, and he was wearing a tweed jacket, jeans, and a crisp shirt. He looked like a bit of an academic.

We talked for a few moments, but I had no intention of getting involved with another man—not for a good long time, anyway—so I went off and hung around with Sarah, over by the stage.

"Who's that guy with the big nose?" she asked me. "He keeps staring at you. He looks like a love-struck puppy."

"No idea," I replied.

An hour later, I once again found myself chatting with him just outside the barn—his name was Simon Shore, he was a fine arts dealer—and he was really a very funny guy. As we talked, the weather began to turn a bit cold, and Simon removed his tweed jacket and slipped it over my shoulders. I remember being very impressed. *What a perfect gentleman,* I thought. *And not bad-looking either.* By the end of the evening, we'd swapped numbers, and the next day, determined not to waste any time, he called. We went out to dinner and he made me laugh, which I really liked. I hadn't really thought of him as a romantic possibility, but he was funny and sweet and decent and I suddenly saw him in a different light. He told me about his work as a fine arts dealer and I told him about my new job and about my psychic talents. "I don't really believe in that psychic business," he said. "I'm sorry."

"No need for an apology," I said. "I appreciate your honesty."

After dinner, he kissed my cheek like a proper gentleman and told me he'd had a lovely evening. "So did I," I said, and went home to my parents'.

A few days later, Mom was leafing through the *Birmingham Evening Mail* and saw an ad for a singer. I made a call, and the next day I went to Rugby, which is about an hour away, and auditioned for the job. I sang that Celine Dion song again, and another song by an English band called Steps, "One for Sorrow." Happily, I got the job, and the rehearsals started immediately. We rehearsed intensely for a few days, and by week's end I found myself on a small night-club stage with my three bandmates. It was great fun, but certainly not lucrative enough to let me give up my day job.

Meanwhile, Simon and I met for dinner a few more times, and I told him all about Reg. He knew that my wedding had been scheduled for the following weekend, and he handled it like a perfect gentleman. "Why don't you let me take you somewhere nice?" he said. "It'll help you put your mind at ease."

We went to Cheltenham, a beautiful, vibrant little town in Gloucestershire, where we had lunch, went to a movie, and did a little shopping. It was a perfect day . . . until, unbelievably, I spotted Reg's car. I couldn't believe it: He was in Cheltenham the same day! Simon was wonderful. He told me not to worry about it and had me laughing again in no time, and as luck would have it, we didn't run into Reg. By the end of the day I decided I could really trust Simon, and when we returned home the relationship slowly took a more serious turn.

In a matter of weeks I had introduced him to my parents, and he took me round to his place to meet his parents and his sister, Claire. Before long I was practically living with him at his lovely apartment in Stow-on the-Wold, in the Cotswalds. He made me feel like a million dollars.

"You know, the night I met you, before I left the house, I told my mother I was going to meet a man who would change my life," I said.

"I told you I don't believe in that stuff," he said, laughing.

But I believed. And other people believed. And in fact I remember getting a call from my friend Sarah that very week. "I had a client come in this week, and I told her what you had told me about Tony, how he'd been cheating on me, and how every little detail was dead on," she said. "She wants to have a reading with you."

"A reading? I don't do readings."

"No, actually—you do. And I've booked it already. It's next Saturday at noon." She gave me the woman's name and address, then added: "Charge her twenty pounds."

"What?! Twenty pounds? She's a friend of yours. I'm not charging anything."

"Lisa, listen to me. You're good at this. You have to be reimbursed for your time and talent."

On Saturday, feeling somewhat less than confident, I arrived at this lady's house with my Tarot cards and my Psycards. "This is the first reading I've ever done other than for my mother," I said straightaway.

"I know," she said. "Sarah told me, so don't worry. Can I make you a cup of tea?"

"Just water's fine," I said, and she went off to get it.

We sat in her front room, which was full of light, and faced each other across the coffee table. "May I have a personal item?" I asked. She gave me a ring, and I held it for a moment, wondering what I was doing, or who I thought I was fooling. I felt really clueless. But before I knew it I was telling her about her father, whose presence I felt in the room, and who had died of a heart attack—something I couldn't have known. And I told her things about her friends and family, some of whose names actually came to me, and I said she'd be making a change in her job very soon.

"It's uncanny," she exclaimed. "How do you know these things?"

"I don't know," I said. "I'm not sure how, but things just come to me."

She kept urging me to go on, and I tried, but the room felt suddenly empty, as if all the people who had been there, helping me out, had decided to call it a day. "That's all I have for you," I said. "The energy's gone." She seemed very happy with the reading and paid me, but I thought she may have just been being polite.

On my way home, I stopped at Sarah's place to tell her all about it, but found the woman had already rung with her own report. "She thinks you're amazing," Sarah said. "She's going to book another reading and tell all of her friends about you."

"Oh!" I said, pleasantly surprised, wondering what exactly this might mean.

That weekend, Simon and I went off to Scotland for two nights, to have ourselves a little break. It was lovely and I was really starting to feel connected to him. A few weeks later, Simon came to collect me at my parents' house—we were on our way to visit his sister—but my Mom stopped me as I was walking out the door. "You're pregnant," she said.

"I'm not pregnant," I said, laughing but shocked.

"Are you sure?"

"Yes, I'm sure! What made you say such a thing?"

"I know when your time of the month comes, and I have a feeling you're late."

I didn't think it was possible. After all, the doctor had told me it was highly unlikely I'd ever have kids, and I'd already come to accept it.

We drove to see Claire, who was having a few friends over, and she told all the girls that I did psychic readings. "Well, I don't—not really," I protested. But the girls urged me to read for them, and they were so insistent that I gave it a go. I found myself saying, "Someone in this room is pregnant," at which point they all turned to look at the one friend who'd been trying to get pregnant for the better part of a year. "It's you!" they exclaimed. "It's you! It's finally happened!"

I kept talking, unable to help myself: "There's going to be a problem with the pregnancy, but it will be resolved." I looked at the girl in question, and she seemed quite unhappy, but there was nothing to be done about it—that's what I sensed.

The next morning, thinking about the previous evening, and about what my mother had said, Simon and I decided to stop at a pharmacy and purchased a pregnancy kit. We took it back to my parents' place, and I noticed that Simon had never looked more excited. "Do it, then!" he said.

"I can't wee on command!" I said. I think I was just nervous, frankly, not knowing how I would respond to the test, one way or the other, so I couldn't wee all morning. But after lunch I suddenly had the urge. I followed the directions on the kit, then went to join Simon and we waited for that little blue line to appear on the paper strip. It was the longest minute of my life, but then there it was—I was pregnant! I honestly didn't know how to feel about it. Here I was, just beginning to get myself back together, dating a man I didn't really know all that well, and I had new life growing inside me.

Simon's face lit up. "Oh my God," he said. "This is wonderful!" He grabbed his mobile and rang his sister. "Claire," he exulted. "We're pregnant."

I called my friend Sarah and shared the news, but I was filled with self-doubt: "How am I going to take care of a child when I can hardly take care of myself?"

"You don't have to have it," she said.

"No," I said. "I'm keeping it. And it's not an 'it'—he's a boy."

"How do you know?"

"I just do," I said.

"That's spooky!" she said, laughing.

"Yeah," I said. "Some people think so."

I went off to see a doctor, who confirmed the pregnancy, then I broke the news to my mom. We were home, watching *Friends* on the telly, and she was dozing off. Simon was there because I had told him I needed him there for support. During the commercial, Mom woke with a start, yawned, and said she was going to bed.

"I have something to tell you," I said.

"What?" she asked, but she was only half-listening.

"I'm pregnant."

Suddenly she was wide awake. "Oh, Lis," she said, "I knew it."

"Yes, you were right."

"You're not going to keep it, are you?"

"Actually, yes, I am. And it's a him."

"I think you need to think seriously about this before I tell your father," she said, and she went off to bed.

I looked over at Simon. "Well, that went nicely, didn't it," I said.
He didn't know what to say.

For the next few days, my mom was positively dismissive. She kept asking me the same questions over and over again—*Are you sure you're doing the right thing? Do you honestly want to go through with this? Is this the right time to have a baby?*—but at the first sign of morning sickness she became the typical mother. She made sure I had biscuits in the morning to fight the sickness and packed me fresh strawberries every day for lunch, saying they were supposed to quell the nausea. I realized that despite initially being cross about the pregnancy, she was really looking forward to being a grandmother ... even though she warned me, "Don't you dare let that child call me 'Granny.' I'm too young to be a Granny!"

Meanwhile, I started getting calls from complete strangers asking if I'd read for them. They had heard about me from Claire, or from Sarah, or from a friend of a friend of a friend, and they were eager to "book a session." I didn't want to let them down, so I took their numbers and told them I would call them back when I was free. I finally talked to Simon about the possibility of doing readings at the house, of putting my gifts to use, but he was unsupportive and again dismissed the whole thing as quackery. I knew he was wrong, though, so I began returning calls and booking appointments. And that's how it began. Once or twice a week I would arrive at the home of a complete stranger, with my Tarot cards and my Psycards, and the session would get underway. I can't in all honesty say I knew what I was doing, and half the time I didn't even understand what I was saying: "A friend has betrayed you and is desperate to make amends." But *my clients* seemed to understand, which was what mattered, and I was constantly being referred to new people. And that's when I understood: It didn't matter if my reading made no sense to me as long as it made perfect sense to the client. From this point on I understood the importance of not using my logical brain in a reading.

By my second trimester, Simon and I had moved into a house in Redditch, not far from my parents' place, and I began looking at baby clothes. I only ever looked at boys' clothes, and I only ever thought about boys' names, because I just knew my baby was a boy.

By this time I was showing, of course, and I was still working, but looking forward to maternity leave. I was also doing more readings than ever, which I was actually beginning to enjoy. My small successes had given me confidence, and the phone never stopped ringing.

"I wish I could bring clients here," I told Simon.

"No," he said. "I don't want those people in my house." He made fun of me, and of my clients, but not in a mean-spirited way. He simply didn't believe, and that was fine with me. I had no desire to convert him. Plus he had a sense of humor about it. Sometimes he'd come into the bedroom making spooky sounds, keening like a ghost, and he'd put his hand on my belly and say, "Damien? Is that you? Are you in there?"

I was still singing with my little band on the weekends, getting booked into small pubs across the country, or at private parties, and Simon often came to watch, more so as the pregnancy progressed. He was being protective. The doctor urged me to get plenty of bed rest, so I had to stop singing and cut back on my readings. One afternoon, shortly back from the office, I was lying on the couch, feeling miserably large, when I thought back to the night of Claire's party. I had predicted that someone in that room was pregnant, and that there would be problems with the pregnancy. I wondered if perhaps I'd been seeing my own pregnancy. Worried, I called Claire and she made some inquiries. As it turned out, that other girl at the party had indeed been pregnant at the time, but unfortunately she'd lost the baby.

"That's terrible," I said.

"It was," Claire said. "But she's pregnant again. And this time, so far so good."

Photo by Simon Shore

Charlie, age two weeks

"Thank God," I said. "I thought maybe I'd been switching energies from one person to another, which can happen with so many people in the room. I feel like my pregnancy is going to be fine."

My contractions began on a Thursday night, and Simon drove me to the hospital. It soon became apparent, however, that I wasn't ready to give birth, so he left me there and went home. It wasn't until the next day that the contractions began in earnest. On Saturday, April 15, 2000, at 5:10 a.m., Charles Edward Williams-Shore made his appearance. He weighed six pounds fifteen ounces, and he was the handsomest little bugger I'd ever seen.

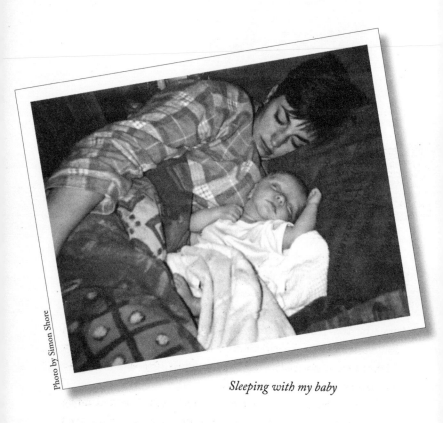

Photo by Simon Shore

Sleeping with my baby

chapter 4

Working Mother

As any mother will tell you, you really only really understand the impact a child has on your life when you have one of your own. Charlie *became* my life. I spent every minute with him, but whenever I had to break away—to shop for food, have my hair done, visit the doctor—I trusted my mom to care for him. Still, I couldn't wait to get back to him. For a time I thought I was being a bit obsessive, but I soon realized I was behaving very much like mothers everywhere.

When Charlie was about four months old, I started doing readings again. Simon was away a great deal, visiting antique fairs all across the country, and I again asked him if I could do the readings at home. "It would make things so much easier on me," I said.

"Absolutely not," he said. "I hate that witchy stuff."

"It used to amuse you," I said.

"I don't mind you doing it, just not in our home."

So off I went, with Charlie in tow. I'd carry him from house to house in his little car seat, scheduling my readings to coincide with his naptimes, and sometimes I'd find myself rocking him under the table with my foot. None of my clients seemed to mind. I'd always start my readings off with a visitation from a spirit. "Your father is making an entrance," I'd say. "Looking very smart in his suit, but he's wearing a flat cap and smoking his pipe." If Charlie got cranky, I'd stop to cuddle him or give him his bottle, but otherwise the reading proceeded smoothly.

One evening, I gave a reading at our house against Simon's explicit directions, but he was out of town and I was too exhausted to get into my car with Charlie and make the long drive. It was for Eileen, a short, stout Irish lady who had a jolly face and a wonderful sense of humor. Given her many references to God and the saints, she was clearly a devout Catholic. But she was quick to inform me that she was a Reiki master, which meant that she was very much part of my world too. I'd heard a little about Reiki, whose practitioners believe we are all sustained by a life force, and that from time to time it falls into disharmony. "Reiki is a sort of spiritual tune-up," Eileen explained. "You should think about getting into it. You're gifted. Gifted people are usually very good at it."

We sat down to do the reading, and the first thing I told Eileen was that there would be big changes at work.

"Fucking hell!" she bellowed in her broad Irish accent. "You're right. I hate that bleeding place! Only last week I decided I was moving on!" She was not only built like a trucker, she swore like one, God bless her.

"I see your daughter's getting married soon," I continued.

"Oooohhhh, bloody hell! That's right, how'd you know that? You're very good, you are! I know you're going to be famous some-day!"

"Oh, I don't know about that," I said.

"But I do," she said. "I've been to lots of readings, and you're spot on, you are! I'm going to have a T-shirt made: I KNEW HER BEFORE SHE WAS FAMOUS."

A few weeks later, Simon was out of town again, and I got a call from a woman who'd once sat with my grandmother. I was able to squeeze her in the next day, but I didn't want to make the drive, so I asked her to come to the house. She arrived precisely on time, which I always appreciate, being a bit of a stickler about punctuality, but as I ushered her inside, I felt a little nervous. She had had a reading with my nan, after all, and I worried about measuring up. I sat her down and took a long look at her. She was about forty-five, and a bit plump, with short, brown hair and what we call a brummie accent—broad and thick, with the local black country dialect.

"I hope you don't expect me to be as good as my nan," I said.

"Oh, don't worry about that," she said. "I've heard many good things about you."

We got off to a good start. I saw some things about her health, and I sensed her late father in the room, and he had a few innocuous messages for her about rather mundane things like the plumbing in her house. But in the middle of the reading, I saw a horrific car accident, the first time I'd ever seen something so grim, and I stopped for a moment and asked her, cautiously, "Do you want me to tell you everything?"

Since we were in the middle of the reading, she knew that I must have seen something quite awful, but she braced herself and pressed me to share it with her. "I'm seeing a car accident," I said. "It's a sports car, blue in color. And your daughter's driving. And it's going to happen this summer, over a long holiday weekend."

She looked totally gone out. "My daughter hasn't got a sports car," she said.

"Well, she's driving it. I can see that clearly."

"But I don't know what you mean. She has a boyfriend, but he hasn't got a sports car either."

"I'm sorry. This is what I'm seeing. And from the looks of it, this could be a fatal accident."

"Can it be avoided?" she asked, and of course she was quite upset.

"Yes," I said. I don't know why I said that, or even if it was me who had said it, because it felt more like a voice in my head had spoken for me. "I'm going to try to give you as much information as I can. That way you might be able to get a sense of when it might happen, and you'll be able to warn your daughter."

"Okay," she said, looking very worried.

"As I said, it's a blue sports car. She's driving with the top down. She's on a long, winding road. There's another road she could have taken, but she made this decision on the spur of the moment, opting for the slower, more scenic route. She prefers this road to the other one. And I can now see that the car is borrowed."

"From whom?"

"I don't know."

"But how can you be so sure about any of this?"

"Because my grandmother is telling me," I said. I don't know why I said that, either, but even as I said it I knew it to be true.

"This has been quite upsetting," the woman said at the end of the reading.

"I'm sorry."

"No, no. It's not your fault. Thank you for being honest with me. I rather wish I didn't have to believe it, but everything else you told me was quite accurate, down to some very small details, so I'm inclined to trust you. Plus so many people have recommended that I see you. That doesn't make me feel any better about it, though."

I don't want to keep you in suspense, so I'll tell the story here. Almost a year later, I had a call from her. "Lisa," she said, "you may not remember me, but I'm the woman you told about the car accident—with the blue sports car and everything."

"Okay," I said, trying desperately to remember because I find

I recall very little of even the most recent readings. She must have sensed this, as she started to explain what I'd told her previously.

"It's the oddest thing. My daughter went to work for a car dealership, and it was a holiday weekend, and she came home in a blue sports car. Then she remembered what I'd told her about the reading, and she called to tell me about the car. She said she and her boyfriend were going to visit friends who lived about an hour away, and she generally took the scenic route, but I told her not to—to take the motorway instead. They stayed about an hour, and on the drive back they took the scenic route, thinking this whole business was really rather silly. But on the trip home she found that all traffic was being diverted into a single lane. A tree had fallen unexpectedly across the road three hours earlier, which is when she would have normally been passing that very spot. This whole thing could have been a coincidence, but I think not. You even had the color of the car right."

"I don't believe in coincidences," I said. "I believe everything happens for a certain reason."

"Well, anyway, I just wanted to thank you," she said. "I believe that reading saved my daughter's life."

"Don't thank me," I said. "I was only the messenger. Thank my nan."

Some months after that reading, and long before the near-accident, Simon and I decided we would like to purchase a property, and we went to look at a house in Webheath, also in Redditch. A pebbled driveway led up to the house, which was just off a main road. It was made of red brick and had lots of charming windows, with ivy climbing all along one side. Right away we christened it Ivy Cottage. The estate agent unlocked the front door and showed us inside. The main room had beautiful stone floors, and an Inglenook fireplace, and an old, homey kitchen—everything you might expect in a charming, English cottage.

"I believe the place was built in the 1820s," the estate agent said.

Simon and I looked at each other. We were grinning. We loved it. We moved in on October 1, 2000, and were settled in within a week. My old rocking chair went perfectly in front of the fireplace, and I wasn't the only one who thought so: There were many nights when I would come downstairs to find the chair rocking, and it would keep rocking when I walked past. I couldn't see anyone in the chair, so I didn't let it bother me. There was also the spirit of a little girl in the house—I could hear her giggling from time to time—but I never saw her, either.

We made it a lovely home, and we were very happy there, but Simon was traveling more often than ever, and Charlie and I were often left alone. Well, *sort of* alone. There was a man in the house. I have no idea who he was, but he'd make his presence known whenever Simon was out of town. I couldn't actually see him, but I could feel his eyes following me around the house, and he'd always be waiting for me at the top of the stairs when it was time for bed.

One night, a short while after tucking Charlie in, I went to bed exhausted and started drifting off to sleep. But I woke moments later, sensing the man's presence more intensely than ever before. I buried my head under the covers, my heart in my throat, until I started to calm down and fell back sleep, only to be awakened a short time later. I woke up feeling as if I were being suffocated. At first I thought it was the covers, but they had fallen to the floor. I tried to move but I was pinned down, and that's when I realized the man, or at least his spirit, was on top of me, trying to have sex. It was crazy! A ghost was trying to have his way with me! I tried to fight him off, but was trapped. I tried to scream but no sound would come out of my mouth. It was like something from a horror film—I must have looked quite a sight, grimacing and pushing against *nothing*—I kept telling him to go to the light, meaning, go to the light of the spirit world. Finally, his hold eased and I managed to get out from under him. I ran into Charlie's room, terrified, quickly closing the door, and I spent the night lying on the floor next to Charlie's cot.

Thankfully, I didn't see the man again that night or the following night, and when Simon returned I didn't say anything. He didn't believe these things anyway. He'd probably laugh at me. And I didn't need that just then. The truth is, things had not been going all that well for us. We'd made a lovely, warm home, and we had a wonderful, healthy son, but we had stopped communicating. I thought perhaps it was my fault, that I'd been focusing too exclusively on Charlie, so I tried doubly hard to engage him, but nothing worked. Simon seemed to have lost interest in me. I began to wonder whether he was keeping something from me, and my first horrible thought was that he was seeing another woman. I didn't want to confront him with false accusations, though, so I kept my feelings to myself.

In the early morning of Christmas Day, about 5 a.m., I couldn't sleep because I had a sinking feeling that something wasn't quite right. I didn't want to spoil the day as we had all sorts of festivities ahead of us, but I needed to know what was wrong—there was something I couldn't put my finger on. I decided to check Simon's mobile phone. I'd like to tell you there was something witchy about it, that a voice in my head told me to do it, but that wouldn't be true. I was just following a woman's instincts, like any other with an awful feeling about her man. But I couldn't find his phone. It wasn't in the kitchen where he normally left it on charge. It wasn't in his trousers. It wasn't on the dining room table. I looked around, frustrated, and that's when the witchy-woo feelings kicked in. I walked toward the front door and reached above the window on the left, and there it was, hidden behind some of the Christmas decorations. I remember trembling, thinking, *Why is his phone hidden? What is going on here?* I looked at the display window and saw he had a new text message, and I opened it, my heart pumping. "I miss you, too, babe," it said. "Merry Christmas. XXX."

All I could think was, *Merry Fucking Christmas to you too, Lisa,* but I was determined to stay calm. It was Charlie's first Christmas, and tears welled in my eyes when I looked at the presents under the tree, but I didn't want to ruin everything by getting into a row with Simon. We'd get through it, I told myself, though God only knew how. I had my mom and dad coming for breakfast later that morning, and in the afternoon we were going to Simon's father and stepmom's house for lunch. I took a deep breath and told myself I'd keep my roiling emotions under control—for the next twelve hours, anyway.

Not surprisingly, it didn't work. I had worked myself up into such a state that within an hour, I walked into our room, carrying Simon's breakfast and Christmas presents and I handed him his phone telling him he had a message. He took one look at it and the blood drained from his face. I stormed out, and he followed me downstairs, in a panic, telling me I had misunderstood. "It's a joke," he said. "It's from a guy I went to university with."

"He calls you 'babe' and sends you kisses?" I said.

"It's a joke, I'm telling you. Guys do that."

I didn't want to get into it because my mom and dad were walking up the road to our house. I opened the door and put on a brave face. *Look how happy we are! It's our first Christmas with our son Charlie, and we're over the moon about it . . . not!*

My parents stayed for a little over an hour and had bacon sandwiches for breakfast along with bucks fizz (champagne and orange juice) and they watched Charlie open his presents. Then they went off to start preparing lunch for my brother and my grandparents. It had been one of the longest hours of my life. I was exhausted. I turned to look at Simon. "I'm not going to your parents' today," I said.

"Please don't do this, Lisa. You don't know how wrong you are."

I ignored him. I went upstairs to put Charlie down for his nap, and when he dozed off I went back downstairs, not knowing how this would play out—or even how I wanted it to play out. Simon was sitting in the kitchen, looking bereft. "Please come to lunch, Lisa," he said.

"I told you already. I'm not going."

"You have it all wrong," he insisted.

"I don't think so. It's clear you're hiding something. I think you're having an affair."

"I'm not having an affair!" he shouted.

"Don't raise your voice to me!" I said, also shouting. "Charlie needs his nap!"

I began to sob, and I honestly didn't know where to turn. Simon kept assuring me that I was wrong, pleading with me, and because I wanted to believe him I let him wear me down. "You and Charlie are everything to me," he said. "I can't believe you'd think otherwise."

So we went to his parents' for the day, and I smiled and laughed my way through it. When we got home, Simon thanked me, and he tried to explain himself again, but I was tired of hearing it and told him so. For the next two days, I wouldn't speak to him—I wouldn't even look at him.

On the third day, December 27, he said he was going to visit his friend Matt in Bristol, and that he would be spending the night.

"I might go to Stevenage for the night," I said, and I mentioned the name of a friend I had long promised to visit.

"Call me when you get there," he said. "Just to let me know you and Charlie got there safely."

When I got to my friend's house, I called Simon, but he didn't answer. I must have called him forty times over the next two hours, and still he didn't answer. Then I put in a call to his friend Matt, who was very surprised to hear from me. "Simon?" he said "Oh yeah, sorry, I haven't heard from Simon in ages."

At that moment, an image popped into my head, and I recognized the place immediately. It was the Lygon Arms, a charming hotel in the Broadway Cotswalds. Simon and I had often driven past it, and for some reason I knew that he was there at that very moment with another woman. I also knew instinctively that our relationship was over. I wanted to drive out there to confront him, but it was snowing heavily, and I had a seven-month-old son to think about, so I decided to stay. But in the morning I called him and told him I knew, and he turned the tables on me and began to shout, "You don't know anything, but you're right—this relationship is over. I can't handle your possessiveness. I told you I wasn't having an affair, and that's the truth."

There were many parties to attend in the days ahead, including a New Year's Eve party at the home of our friends Jonesy and Mike. We put on a brave face and kept our troubles to ourselves, but on the final night of the year I found myself telling Jonesy about the rift. Although Mike and Jonesy were Simon's friends, we had become very close since the birth of Charlie. She was crushed. Like all of our friends, she thought we were very happy together.

"So did I," I said.

"You going to be all right?"

"Yeah. I'll manage. It's Charlie I'm mostly worried about. A boy needs a father."

That night, when I got home, I found a receipt in the car for the Lygon Arms. So Simon *had* been at the Lygon Arms. I wasn't crazy. My senses hadn't failed me.

But sometimes it's awful to be right.

When I again confronted Simon, he didn't even argue. There was nothing to argue about. The relationship was over, and we both knew it, though I suspect he knew it before I did. Men don't have affairs if they're happy.

For the next two months, while I looked for a place to live, we stayed under the same roof and even slept in the same bed. We also sat in front of the computer and worked out our own parental contract. Simon may have failed me as a partner, but he didn't want to fail Charlie as a father and I didn't want him to either.

At the end of February, while Simon was away working, I found a perfect house and moved in over the space of a weekend. When Simon returned from yet another antiques fair, he walked into an empty house.

Immediately following, I found a job as a sales rep for an advertising company. I was back to cold calling, which felt like a giant backward step, but—with a little help from Simon—Charlie and I managed just fine. Still, I became terribly depressed. I became obsessed with Simon. Had he been with other women? How many, and why? And where was he at that very moment? How could he just desert me and Charlie? I became so monomaniacal that I went to see a therapist. "It seems that all my waking moments are consumed by Simon," I said. "Getting at the truth about Simon, finding out where he is and what he is doing."

"And what would that accomplish?" he asked.

He had a point, but it didn't help. I think I wanted to hate Simon, but I couldn't hate him. In fact, I wanted him back. I felt the failure of the relationship was somehow my fault, not his, and I wanted another chance to make things right. *These things happen,* I told myself. *Life isn't perfect. And Charlie needs his parents.* But in fact I was thinking about my own future as a single mother. I was convinced no one would ever take me on again; that I'd had my chance and blown it.

One day after work, I fetched Charlie from childcare, as I did five days a week. I put him into his car seat and as we headed home in silence, I found myself suddenly enveloped by a crushing, black cloud of depression. I was driving down a very busy road that had a T-junction at one end, with a brick wall dead ahead. I was supposed to make a left, toward home, but suddenly I thought I should drive straight into the wall and be done with it. I began to speed up, mindlessly committed to the idea, but just then Charlie laughed from the backseat. It was a big, warm, happy-to-be-alive laugh, and I realized I had to get through this, if only for him. So I slowed down and made the left, and we went home. When I tucked Charlie in that night, I promised I would take care of him forever.

At this point, I wasn't doing any readings—I was far too messed up to even think about it—but I became obsessed with having readings of my own. Like most people who go to readings, I was looking for answers, peace of mind, direction. The first reading I went to was quite memorable. There was a woman in Lichfield with a fantastic reputation, and she was able to squeeze me in one Sunday afternoon. I left Charlie with Mom and made the forty-minute drive to her place, and the moment I took my seat she said, "You just split up with a man. His name—hmm, let me think. . . . I believe it might be Simon."

"Bloody hell," I said. I was completely blown away. She had come up with his name straightaway! I mean, I knew this stuff is real, but I had never taken it for granted—and I still don't.

"Now, I know you're worried, dear," she went on, "but I want you to stop worrying. You two are getting back together."

"We are?!"

"Absolutely," she said.

She went on tell me all sorts of other things that weren't quite as accurate, but her mistakes didn't alter my first impression. I wanted her to be right about Simon. We *were* getting back together. Charlie would be growing up with his family under one roof. I became so obsessed with our fated reconciliation that I went to more and more readings, desperate to confirm what the first woman had told me. At one point, I was having four or five readings a week, spending money I didn't have on psychics who claimed to have an ability, or calling the psychic hotlines, running up hundreds of pounds in charges.

One night, I called a psychic hotline I had called several times before and was greeted by a very friendly lady, who told me to tell her when to stop shuffling the cards, which I did. She explained that she was laying the cards out and she started reading them. I heard her flip some pages and realized she was reading the meanings from a book! I couldn't believe it; this was not how a genuine psychic would work.

"Are you reading all this from a book?" I surprised myself by asking.

"Erm, yes, and it tells me that—"

I put the phone down straightaway, that was enough of that! I didn't trust psychic hotlines, and I should have listened to my friends who were all telling me it was a waste of money.

Then one day, I was listening to the tape of the reading that the psychic in Lichfield had given me—the one where I was convinced she had told me that Simon and I were getting back together. I listened properly to what the psychic had told me, and I realized that she had never said anything about reconciliation. I'm the one who had guided the conversation. I'm the one who had pushed her to tell me what I wanted to hear. I wanted so much to get back together with Simon that I wouldn't listen to anything that suggested otherwise. I felt like a complete fool, but the lesson wasn't wasted. I vowed that I would never let myself be led by a client. Wishful thinking is all well and good, but honesty is the better option. I would tell only what I was being told, even if it disappointed my clients—even if they were hoping to hear something else entirely.

The experience shook me up in other ways too. I realized I had to move forward. I began to reach out to old friends I could trust, as my therapist had once suggested, and connected with Susan, with whom I'd worked at Graveneys, the sports shop in Redditch—the one with whom I'd discovered boys and nightclubs. By this time, so many years later, she was a single mom herself, with a boy of six, working part-time as a hairdresser, but unlike me she wasn't wallowing in misery. She was dating and enjoying life, and her attitude helped me understand that life moved forward, with or without me, and that it was up to me to make the best of it. I was immediately transformed. It was the kind of transformation one only sees in movies. And even my therapist was impressed. "You've made me a very dramatic turnaround in the last week," he said. "Would you care to tell me about it?"

"I don't know where to begin," I said, grinning. I was quite impressed with myself, and delighted that he'd noticed the change. "I was spending a small fortune on psychics, trying to get them to tell me all sorts of wonderful things about my future, and being a complete idiot about it. Then I ran into an old girlfriend who has managed to make a very nice life for herself, single motherhood notwithstanding."

"Remarkable, isn't it? The good things that come our way when we open our eyes."

"Yes," I said. "It is."

"What else is going on?"

"Charlie's first birthday's coming up soon," I said. "I want it to be very special, and I'm trying to sort out what to do."

The one detail I didn't share with my therapist was the fact that I'd been thinking about having Charlie christened. I don't know why I didn't share it with him, but perhaps it's because I hadn't been christened myself, so I didn't want to come across like a hypocrite—a lesson I'd learned from my dad. I ended up going to see my granddad to discuss it. "What if I got christened too?" I said. "Then it wouldn't be hypocritical, would it?"

"Lisa," he said, "if you feel it's the right thing to do, it *is* the right thing to do."

It reminded me of what my nan had told me about readings: *Trust your gut instinct. It will never let you down.*

"That's very good advice, Granddad," I said. I studied him. He was eighty-two years old at the time, but still did fifty sit-ups and push-ups a day, and was healthy and fit. I thought back to the many summers we'd spent together in the caravan, and to the day—much

Charlie and Mommy

more recent—when he'd held Charlie in his arms. He was the first member of my family to hold Charlie, and he was absolutely besotted with him. "I'm going to hang on as long as I can just to enjoy this little bugger," he'd told me.

He'd said plenty of other things to me over the years, part of his quiet effort to give me a little guidance, and that day he said two more. The first was "Lisa, if you can't have at least one good belly laugh a day, you're not happy." And the other was "Lisa, never get to my age and say 'What if?' Get to my age and say 'I did it and I don't regret it.'"

Immediately after that visit, I got busy arranging the christening. I lived a stone's throw from a Church of England church, and Charlie and I went over and met with the reverend. A few days later, he came over for a cup of tea. He settled in, the cup resting on his knee, and we had a pleasant little chat. I even told him about my long-ago experience with the Sunshine Group, and my short-lived "religious awakening."

"How do you feel about God now?" he asked.

"I'm not sure," I said. "I've always believed that there was something higher than us, but I don't know if it's God exactly—or what that even means. But I truly believe that there is something."

He smiled at me. It was the nicest smile in the world. "Lisa, you have a belief, and that's all I ask for." It was really lovely. I almost felt like crying. "When do you want to do this?" he asked.

"Well, Charlie's birthday is on the fifteenth of April," I said.

"Perfect!" he said. "Easter Sunday. Let's do it then. In the Bible, that's when everyone gets rebaptized anyway, so we couldn't ask for better."

With only weeks to go, I sent out a few invites. I invited Charlie's dad, and his family, of course, but unfortunately—or unsurprisingly, depending on how you want to look at it—none of them could make it. I invited my parents and grandparents. My brother was godfather, and he came with his wife. Various friends showed up, including Mike and Jonesy, who were also godparents.

On April 15, 2001, everyone gathered at my place, and we made the short walk to the church together. We attended the regular Easter Sunday service, and toward the end the reverend performed our joint christening. It was brief and elegant and quite heartwarming—for me, if not for everyone else. Then we walked back to the house and had a little party for Charlie, and the very first present he opened was a drum. It was a gift from my mom. I looked at her and shook my head in horror, but I was smiling. "Thanks a lot, Mom," I said. "I'll bring this to your house when he comes to visit."

I have a lovely photograph from that day. It shows my grandfather, my father, my brother, and my son—four generations of men in my family. It's a very special photograph, and I keep it close to this day. The drum, on the other hand, is long gone, for which I am truly grateful. For weeks afterward, Charlie drove me mad with his banging.

In the weeks and months following Charlie's birthday, my friend Susan seemed more determined than ever to whip me into shape. I had lost a lot of weight from the stress of the breakup, and she made sure I ate properly. Then one day she sat me down in front of a mirror in her house and said, "We need to do something about your hair!"

We studied my reflection in the mirror and I was horrified by the lifeless, brown bob that looked as boring as I felt I'd become.

"What are we going to do about it, then?" she asked.

"Haven't got a clue," I said.

"Right, then. Leave it to me."

Photo by Lisa Williams

The four generations of "Williams" men

She cut it short and spiky, then decided it would look even better if she dyed it different colors. The result was startling but rather fun. "I love it," I said in an unconvincing tone.

But I *did* come to love it. People noticed me on the streets and smiled. Men flirted with me. Shop clerks made pleasant remarks. I began a slow transformation, which started at the top of my head—with my hair—and worked itself down to the very tips of my toes. Suddenly, I understood why women made such a fuss about their hair. It really *did* have the power to change your life (or at least how you *felt* about your life). I went from shame at being a single mom to *embracing* it. I was standing on my own two feet. I was earning a living and taking good care of my little boy, and in my heart I knew I was destined for great things. I began to look around for a new job and applied for a position as an office manager at another advertising company. "What can you do?" the woman asked me.

"Anything," I said.

Again, I got hired on the spot. I was feeling good about myself, and the feeling traveled. I absolutely radiated positivity.

Shortly after I settled into the new job, I got back into my readings. Some of my clients had given up hope of ever sitting with me again, but most of them had never stopped calling. I began with two or three readings during the week in the evenings after work, and another two or three on weekends, and before long I was being flooded with requests.

Funny thing, that. At my lowest point, I'd felt lost and abandoned, as if life had somehow betrayed me. But with a little perspective, I realized I'm the one who had lost my way, I'm the one who'd abandoned hope, and I can tell you—it felt damn good to be back.

Oddly enough, it was my readings that helped me find my way. Clients would come to me with their stories, some of them quite tragic, and it really put my life into perspective. I realized that we are all shaped by our past, the good and bad alike, and that we needed to be thankful for those experiences. I also realized that one was powerless to change the past, and it taught me a lesson I hold dear to this day: Let it go. Be happy now. Keep moving.

Photo by Kevin Harris

Life as a medium

chapter 5

Talking to the Dead

In July 2001, shortly after I'd arrived for work one morning, my mobile rang. Before I'd even fished it out of my bag, I knew it was bad news about my grandfather.

"Hello?"

"Lisa, it's your nan."

"Granddad's in the hospital, isn't he," I said.

There was a brief pause. "Yes," she said. "How did you know?"

"What happened?" I asked.

"They think it was an asthma attack and he has a slight chest infection. They've taken him to Selly Oak Hospital and he's on a respirator, but he's doing fine, he'll be okay."

"I can't make it today. I'm at work, and I've got Charlie tonight. Do you think he will mind if I visit first thing tomorrow morning?"

"That'll be fine, dear. He should only be there for a few days, anyway. He'll be so happy to see you as soon as you can make it."

The following morning, early, I dropped Charlie at my parents' and drove down to the hospital. As I parked the car, I remember feeling a huge weight on my shoulders, an actual, physical weight, and it grew heavier as I moved toward the entrance. I tried to figure out what it meant, and at first I assumed it had something to do with my nan, who had died at that very hospital a few years earlier. But deep down I knew it was connected to my grandfather, and it occurred to me—on a deep, witchy level—that things were far more serious than anyone realized.

I found my way to the ward, and my grandmother was standing next to his bed fussing over him as she always did. And Dad was in a chair beside the bed. They were both smiling brightly, and he was no longer on the respirator. "Look at him," Nan said. "He looks so much better today. He's already flirting with the nurses and telling jokes. He'll be having a party after we leave. And the doctor says he's in such good shape they're going to let him go home tomorrow."

I went over and kissed my granddad, and he smiled up at me, his head framed by the pillows. "It's nice of you to have come, but I'm fine," he said, trying to look bright and happy.

My nan excused herself and went off to use the loo. Dad went to get a drink, so I pulled the chair closer to the bed. "You know that stack of racing forms in the dining room—the mess that your nan's always on to me about?" he said. I did know. My grandfather fancied himself a bit of a gambler, and he liked to bet on the horses. He was forever adding to his endless stacks of horse-related literature, studying the racing forms. "Well, I've cleaned it up!" he added.

"I'll believe that when I see it!" I said.

"You'll be real proud of me," he said, laughing.

"I'm proud of you now," I said.

Then he winked playfully and said, "You know where everything is, right?"

I was about to ask him what he meant, but Nan was back from

her visit to the loo, and the moment passed. We made a little small talk, then my dad returned and before long I had to leave to fetch Charlie from Mom's. "I'll come by the house Monday when you're out," I said. "With Charlie."

"That would be nice," he said. "Give the little man a kiss from me."

I looked into his eyes—they were a lovely, deep blue—and I wanted so much to tell him that I loved him, but we weren't like that in our family. We had feelings, of course, but we didn't go around sharing them, and I knew it would have sounded a tad theatrical to express what was in my heart. So I gave him a little kiss and left the room.

My nan followed me out, beaming. "He looks good, doesn't he?" And I turned to her and said, "Nan, there's worse to come." I couldn't help myself—the words just came out of me. But she wouldn't hear it. "No, no, no," she said. "He's going to be fine. The doctor said so. It'll be ever so nice to have him back home."

I didn't want to argue with her, so I kissed her good-bye and returned to the car park and got into my car. I began to cry straight-away. I knew I would never see my grandfather alive again. Every-one else, the doctors included, seemed to think he was on the mend, but I was convinced they were all wrong.

The next day, Sunday, my dad phoned to say that my grandfa-ther had taken a slight turn for the worse, and that he'd be staying in the hospital for another day or two. "But don't worry," he added. "He's going to be okay."

The following day, Monday morning, at five a.m., I bolted awake, my heart racing. For the next two hours, I felt increasingly irritable, and I was pacing the house like a caged beast, waiting to get on with what was likely to be a miserable day. At 7:30, just as I was about to wake Charlie and get him ready for nursery, there was a light knock at the front door. It was my mom, looking ashen. She said simply, "Your granddad died."

"When?" I asked.

"Less than three hours ago. At five o'clock."

Five o'clock? That's when I'd woken up.

"Why didn't you call me?" I asked.

"It was just the three of us there," she said. "Your dad, Nan, and myself. We got called back to the hospital at one a.m. They said they didn't think he was going to make it through the night, and you had Charlie, so we didn't want you to worry."

I thought back to that psychic in Welwyn Garden City, the one who had told me my grandfather would die with three people at his bedside. Unfortunately, she was right that I wasn't one of them.

"You all right?" Mom asked.

"I had an awful feeling about this," I said.

"I'm going to have to tell your brother."

"I'll do it; you go and get some rest," I said.

Mom left, and I went upstairs and got Charlie ready, then dropped him at nursery. From there, I drove to Christian's house in a complete daze; I was running on autopilot. Both he and his wife were working nights, and I knew they had probably only just gone to bed. He showed up at the door, rubbing the sleep from his eyes, surprised to see me there. I walked in and I broke the news to him. After recovering from his initial shock, he got dressed and we drove to my nan's house.

"I knew he was going to die," I said en route.

"Yeah, whatever," he said.

I looked over at him. He was practically sneering. My brother is the biggest nonbeliever in the world.

"Yeah," I said. "When I left the hospital Saturday, I knew I'd never see him again."

"Easy to say that now," he said through the tears he was fighting to hide.

I didn't answer. This was no time for silly arguments.

When we got to Nan's house, she was putting on a brave face, but deep down I saw her hurt—she had just lost the love of her life.

We hugged and tried to make ourselves useful. I went to put on another pot of tea, and Christian went out into the garden to have a cigarette. As I was preparing the tea, it struck me that, for the English, tea seems to be the answer to everything. Someone has a problem. *Make a nice cup of tea.* Someone dies. *Make a nice cup of tea.* Personally, I could have done with a cup of hot chocolate. Chocolate makes everything right for me.

Just as the kettle started to boil, my brother burst back into the house, looking spooked. "You will never believe it, but he just spoke to me!"

"Who?"

"Granddad!"

"That doesn't surprise me," I said, trying not to smile. "What did he say?"

"He said, 'Hello, Christian.' I didn't wait around to hear the rest."

"There you go," I said, amused.

"Lisa, you don't understand. I don't want him to speak to me. You're the one who speaks to the dead—you're the freaky one. I don't believe in this stuff."

"Would you like a cup of tea?" I said, nonchalantly.

"Why don't you do something?"

"What do you want me to do?" I said. "I know he's here and I suspect he'll be talking to me soon."

"I can't cope with this," he said, shaking his head.

I went over and gave him a hug, and I looked over his shoulder at Granddad's lovely garden. I had spent much of the first year of my life out there, sitting in my high chair on clear days, watching Granddad tend to his plants. "Well," I said. "Now do you believe in what I do?"

"Of course not," he said, and we both laughed.

I took Nan her tea, and a short while later my parents arrived, followed by more relatives and loads of friends. It was like a tea party, with people spilling out into the garden and reminiscing about good old Jack.

"No one knows where his papers are," Nan wailed. "He was sorting out the racing magazines in the dining room a couple of weeks ago, but the papers that really matter—I can't find them anywhere. I can't even remember if it's a burial he wants, or a cremation."

"Cremation," I said.

"How do you know?" she asked me.

"He told me," I said.

My brother gave me one of his looks.

"Maybe he wrote something about it in his wallet," Nan said. "But his wallet's in the hospital."

"No, it's not. It's here. And he wrote nothing about it in his wallet."

"It must be at the hospital. I've looked everywhere," Nan insisted.

"It's in that drawer," I said, indicating where she should look. She opened the drawer and there it was. She held it up and turned to look at me. "Your grandfather always had this with him. How did you know it was here?" she asked.

"He told me," I said.

"Like he told you about the cremation?" my brother said, scoffing.

"Listen, if I can tell you exactly what's in his wallet, will you believe me about the cremation?" They all looked at me, ready to take up the challenge. My dad took the wallet from Nan's hand. "There's a five-pound note," I said. Sure enough my dad pulled it out. "There's also one pound forty-seven in change," I said. My dad poured the change into his hand and counted it. I was off by three pence. "There's a little picture of Charlie right next to his British Legion card," I went on, and I was right again. "Now will you believe that I can speak to him and he wants a cremation?"

They all stared at me. Nan finally broke the silence. "Okay," she said, her voice just a notch above a whisper. "Cremation it is. But who's going to pay for it?"

"He's got insurance," I said confidently.

"No, he doesn't. I've got insurance, but we let his lapse."

"Nan, you're wrong." Guided by my granddad, I began pulling papers out of the drawers. It didn't take me long before I had the right documents in hand, and I turned to face them. They were all staring at me, gobsmacked. It was the first time they'd seen me in action, so to speak.

"You're just like Airplane Nanny," Mom said.

"I wish," I said.

"I always thought I was the one with the insurance," Nan said, still struggling to get her mind around what had just happened.

"You'll have to take care of the garden now," I told her. "You know how he loved his roses."

"Oh, I will," she said.

"Hold on," I said, cocking my head to one side, listening. "It's Granddad. He's telling me he wants me to sing at the funeral." They were staring at me. "That does sound a little self-serving, doesn't it?"

"Is he here?" Nan asked.

"Yes. I can't see him," I said. "But I can hear him."

"He always liked that Celine Dion song," she said.

"'My Heart Will Go On.'"

"And you'll have to sing something by Perry Como."

"No," I said. "He's telling me Bette Midler. "He wants 'Wind Beneath My Wings.' And hold on . . . he also wants 'The Way We Were,' by Barbra Streisand." They were staring again. "Don't look at me," I said. "*I'm* not picking them."

In the days ahead, I was busy making arrangements for the funeral, and I decided I didn't want to break down crying in mid-song. Plus I didn't want to be the center of attention. The funeral was about my granddad, not me, so I decided to go to a friend's recording studio to make a CD.

It was a lovely service, and totally packed. My granddad had more friends than any of us had ever imagined, and he certainly deserved them. At the end of the service when "Wind Beneath My Wings" started to play, the curtains closed and the coffin disappeared from view.

It was one of the hardest days of my life. I had held it together for my nan, but by the time I got home I felt so wrung out I didn't think I'd ever recover.

The next morning, I was still in a terrible state, and if it wasn't for Charlie, I wouldn't have found the energy to drag myself out of bed. I fed Charlie, got him dressed, and dropped him at nursery, still feeling hollowed out. I really struggled to make it through work. At the end of the day, I got into my car and began sobbing again, but a moment later I stopped. I had a feeling that Granddad was in the car with me, urging me to pull myself together, and to keep doing what I'd been born to do. It wasn't anything specific—I didn't see him, and he wasn't talking to me—but he was definitely communicating, and it made me feel good. Also, since I knew I hadn't been put on the planet to make cold calls, I assumed he was referring to my psychic gifts.

In short order, I got back to my readings, and one of the very first was with Janey, a single mom, like myself. It was a Friday, and I'd gone over with Charlie. She had a son about his age and they lived in a mobile home that was parked on her father's property. Soon the two boys had fallen asleep on the bed and I began the reading. "Your home isn't going to be here for much longer," I said.

"But it's been here for years," she said. "Where's it going to go?"

"I don't know, but a bungalow is going to take its place. And it's actually higher up."

"On the hill, you mean?"

There was a hill just behind the mobile home, and all of the property belonged to her dad. "No," I said. "Just higher. I can't explain it any better than that."

"What else?" she said.

"You're going to be working for yourself someday."

"No, I'm not," she said. "I can't see myself leaving the family business."

I mentioned a few other things, and she couldn't relate to any of those, either, but she listened openly, without judgment. After the reading we chatted about life as single mums and realized we had more in common than just the boys. We had a lovely evening, and when I eventually looked at my watch, I realized it was late, and I had to get Charlie home to bed. She tried to pay me for the reading but I refused to take her money, knowing from experience that it wasn't easy trying to make ends meet as a single mother. And while she was happy with the reading, and with many of the things I'd said, I felt it hadn't been one of my best.

Photo by Nykki Hardin

Janey and Lisa

Janey and I have remained friends to this day and—as it turned out—her father sold the business years later, and she went to work for herself. Her parents got rid of the mobile home and built a bungalow on the property, but they built up the foundations, so it was raised, almost looking down at the spot where the mobile home had been, just as I had said it would be.

There were many readings during this period, some of which I was doing at home. It was easier, what with Charlie and all, and it kept me from driving all over the place. I remember one involving Lucy, a sweet, good-natured woman of about thirty-five. We were in the middle of talking about her grandmother, who had passed recently, when out of the blue I found myself telling her about an accident. "It will be a freak accident," I said. "A little girl is going to die."

"But I don't have a little girl," Lucy said, alarmed.

"No," I said. "She's not your little girl. And you're not going to be directly affected. In fact, I'm not sure you even know the girl, but I believe you'll know her mother, or someone who is close to her mother."

"Do you see anything else?"

"No," I said. "I'm not seeing any names or anything. But I think she has blond hair."

There's more to the story, but this time I think I'll keep you in suspense.

I even did unscheduled, unsolicited readings—completely by accident. Once I was at Tesco's, shopping for groceries, and found myself at the checkout line, mesmerized by the young clerk. She noticed me staring and said, not unkindly, "What are you looking at?"

"I'm sorry," I said. "But I was wondering: Do you believe in spirits and mediums and clairvoyants, stuff like that?"

"Actually, I do, yes."

"Well, I'm not in the habit of approaching complete strangers, but your mother is standing just behind you." She turned around, saw nothing there, then looked over at me again, wary. "She passed recently of cancer, didn't she?" I said. She nodded, numb. "She wants you to know that she knew you were at her bedside. She heard you say good-bye."

The poor girl struggled to find the words. "I can't believe you just said that," she managed at last. "It's true, I wasn't sure she'd heard me. I thought I'd arrived too late."

"That necklace is hers, isn't it?" I said. "And you put it on today because the day has some significance."

"Yes," she said, astonished. "It's her birthday."

"Well, she just smiled, so I assume she's having a good one."

The girl came around from behind the counter and gave me a big hug. "Thank you so much," she said, beginning to cry. "You have no idea how much that means to me."

In general, my readings seemed to be getting stronger. I think this was partly because my life was in a better place. I'd survived the split with Simon and discovered I could manage quite nicely on my own. And I'd learned a thing or two about myself in therapy, notably that I had to let go of the past. I was one of those people who seemed to wallow in their mistakes, real or imaginary, and I was learning to move forward, learning to clear out the junk. As a result, everything in my life had seemed somehow brighter and clearer.

At that stage in my career, I felt that sharing these otherworldly messages with my clients, and offering them a bit of guidance, was my main job as a psychic. I didn't tell them where to go, or what to do with their lives, but I shared the information I'd gleaned in the reading, and hoped it would be of some use when they made decisions about their respective futures. We might talk about relationships, work, physical health—whatever came up. I never knew what to expect, and neither did they. What's more, I often told them things that made absolutely no sense to me, but which seemed to make sense to them, if not then and there, during the reading, then at some later point. I can't tell you how many times I would hear back from a client, days, weeks, or even years later, with a variation on a theme: "You know that thing you told me about, such-and-such or so-and-so? Well, it just came true!"

In those early days, I was focused exclusively on my skills as a psychic. When the client arrived, we would chat for a moment or two, and then I'd direct them to my reading table, push the record button on my tape player, and get started. I always record every reading and give my client the tape, or CD as it is now. The readings lasted about an hour, and I would always do a little protection before we started, and then I would ask for help from the spirit world. I passed on the information that I was getting, and I only asked them to verify that I was on the right track, or if they could relate to the message, and at the end I gave the client an opportunity to ask questions. As I got more deeply into it, however, I discovered that the spirits had their own agendas, and that I would do well to let them guide things along, so I began to operate as more of a medium. I found myself in this nether territory between the real world and the spirit world, with the client on one side and the dead on the other, and some of the dead had plenty to say. It made sense to listen, particularly since they seemed to know a lot more than I did. I didn't abandon the cards, of course, but it became increasingly clear that the best answers were coming from the other side—from the dead, who had long been clamoring for my attention. This, then, is where I began to put my greatest efforts. I would talk to the dead.

One evening, a new client came in, and a spirit appeared before we'd even started. "I have your father here," I said. She looked confused. "Your father's dead, isn't he?" I said, with as much conviction as I could muster. She nodded. "Well, he's already made an entrance." Now she looked more alarmed than confused. "Surely you knew I spoke to dead people?" I ventured.

"What does he look like?" she asked.

"He's about five-foot-eight, he's wearing a suit, and he has glasses and a comb-over hairstyle."

"That's him," she said.

"That's odd," I said, studying him. She turned to look, but of course she saw nothing. "He's standing at the foot of the stairs, licking his forefinger and turning the pages of an imaginary book."

"What book?" the woman said.

He flipped another page. "What's that book you're reading?" I asked.

"The Bible," he answered.

I turned to my client. "He says he's reading the Bible." She looked absolutely stunned. I turned back to her father. "What are you looking for?"

"I'm trying to find where it says you're doing the work of the Devil," he said, but he was smiling like an imp.

"*Me?*" I said. "You're in spirit. You're the dead person. You're the one who showed up, so why is it the work of the Devil?"

At this point he'd found what he was looking for, because suddenly he was quoting scripture to me. "Here it is," he said. "Leviticus, 19:31. 'Do not turn to mediums or seek out spiritists, for you will be defiled by them. I am the Lord your God.'"

"Defiled? Nobody's being defiled here."

"Here's another one," he said, flipping to the next page. "Leviticus, 20:27. 'Men and women among you who act as mediums or psychics must be put to death by stoning.'"

"That's horrid," I said. "That sounds like Old Testament talk. I'm somewhat familiar with the Bible, but I don't believe there's death by stoning in the new version."

"What are you talking about?!"

I turned to look at my client. She had been listening to a very one-sided conversation, since she couldn't hear her father. "I'm sorry," I said. "He seems to think that this is the work of the Devil."

"This is all very strange," she said. "A couple of minutes ago, when we first sat down, and you told me that my father was here, I didn't believe you. He's a born-again Christian. He's the last person

I expected to come through, but now it makes sense." She was smiling now. "I can't wait to tell my mom. I'll see if she'll book a reading, and I know my sister will want to see you for sure."

That same week, exhausted, I went to bed right after I'd tucked Charlie in, which seldom happened. I was lying there, semiconscious, with my eyes closed, when suddenly I saw a woman directly in front of me. She was young, with long, blond hair, pulled back into a ponytail, and she seemed to be floating in the air directly in front of me. But of course my eyes were still closed, so I was only seeing her in my mind's eye, or my Third Eye, which is centered about an inch above the brows. Suddenly I realized it was my grandmother, Airplane Nanny, but a long-ago version of her. The image began to float around the bed, and it kept changing, and I saw her at various stages of her life. I was wary, not knowing what it meant, but I wasn't frightened. On the contrary, I was very happy to see her.

"Lisa," she said. "I have something to tell you."

I slowly opened my eyes and there she was, just like I saw her in my mind's eye. I tried to answer, if only to greet her, but for some reason I couldn't speak. My hands were on top of the covers, and they suddenly felt freezing cold. Under the covers, however, my body remained warm.

I thought out my answer, loudly: "What is it?"

"I've taken you this far, and I can't take you any further," she said. She turned and gestured, and the figure of a young man floated out of the shadows and came to rest by her side, hovering there. All I could think was, *He looks like a young Neil Diamond*. I know it sounds ridiculous, but it's the truth. He was about thirty, with beautiful, thick, dark hair, and a light-olive complexion, and he was wearing a black turtleneck.

"This is Ben," Nan said. "He'll be here for you from now on."

"Where are you going?" I thought.

As if she heard me she answered, "I'm not going anywhere. I will help you when you need me, but Ben will take you further."

At that moment, they both instantly disappeared. I shut my eyes tight and begged them to come back, but nothing happened. I lay there for a long time, pleading with them to return, but I eventually fell asleep and I slept soundly till morning.

When I awoke, I wondered if the whole thing had been a dream, and in fact I dismissed it as such. I gave Charlie his breakfast, dropped him at nursery, and returned home to do a reading for a woman named Carole, a friend of my friend Janey's. This wasn't the first time I'd met her—I had read for her before—but this time she had brought one of her friends along. As soon as we started the reading, the name "Josh" popped into my head, and a moment later the Neil Diamond look-alike was in the room, sitting in the armchair by the window. "Josh!" I said. "I can't believe it's you! I thought last night was a dream."

"No, it wasn't a dream," he said, smiling. "And my name isn't Josh. It's Ben."

"Oops! I'm sorry," I said, also smiling. He was not only handsome, he had a good sense of humor. "I promise I'll remember."

"Ask Carole about Bill," he said.

"Okay," I said.

"Hello?!" Carole said. She looked very confused.

"I'm sorry," I said. "I was having a conversation with a gentleman I only just met last night, and he says I should ask you about Bill."

She thought for a second, then said, "I had a cousin, Bill; he died unexpectedly."

Bill then began speaking through Ben, and Carole had a wonderful reading. Before she left, she booked another reading for herself in six months' time. Ben, however, was much less predictable than my clients. I couldn't summon him or make an appointment to speak with him. I sometimes wished I had a magic telephone so I could chat with him. He showed up when he wanted to, and I often wondered why he had turned up at all. Sometimes he just waved from across the room, then floated off. And on more than one occasion, he'd make remarks about my clients. "Oh, she's a looker, that one! Love those legs!" I thought this was bad behavior for a spirit guide, and I told him so, but we had a good laugh about it.

Occasionally he'd show up in the middle of the day, at the oddest times. I'd be doing dishes or putting away the laundry, and there he was, looking as if he had all the time in the world, which I guess he did. On those occasions, I pressed him to explain the role he was to play in my life, but he never answered directly, he would just say something cryptic. "You'll see," he might say. Or, "I'll be there when you need me."

And he contradicted himself too. He once told me we had shared several lives together, and that I'd chosen him to be my spirit guide in the course of one of them, but not long after he said that Nan had picked him to look out for me. Whenever I asked him for details about my own past lives—*Was I burned to death in a fire? Was I once mauled to death by dogs? Could he explain where my fear of the water had come from?*—he'd smile but refuse to answer. And if I asked about his own history, he *still* refused to answer.

On Friday, September 7, 2001, I was at work, and I had a call on my mobile from Daniel Moss, who had done one previous reading with me, months earlier, and interestingly, was in fact one of my few male clients. He was very businesslike: "Lisa, it's Dan Moss. I need to see you. It's urgent."

I set a meeting for the following day, and Daniel arrived right on time, as always. He had come from his home, and all he'd brought with him was his mobile phone.

"Okay, Dan, what's so urgent?" I said.

"I'm off on a business trip shortly, and I need your advice on certain matters," he said, impatient to get on with it.

"Do you want to know everything?" I asked. This phrase had become habit. I'd learned early on to ask the question before we sat down. If I asked it in the middle of the reading, the client would know that I had seen something decidedly unpleasant, at which point I'd be forced to tell them, regardless.

"Yes," he said.

I asked him for a personal item—he gave me his watch—and I plunged in: "You're going to New York, but I don't think it's a good time to go," I said.

"I have to go," he said.

"I'm not going to tell you what to do, but if you do decide to go I'm going to ask you to be careful."

"Why? What do you see?"

"I'm not sure. I see your son trying to reach you, there's a distressed phone call from him."

"Has he done something at school?"

"No. It's not about him. He's just very keen to get hold of you."

"I don't know what that means."

"I don't either," I said. "But I see a lot of devastation and destruction around you. It's as if the world is coming down around your ears."

"Well, that's very reassuring, isn't it?" he said, joking, but I could see he was worried. "Could you be more specific?"

"No," I said. I'd seen an image, briefly—dust, flames, destruction—but a cloud had swept it all away. "I see, however, that you're going to get into a terrible traffic jam on your way to Heathrow, and you're going to worry about missing your flight."

"I'm leaving for Heathrow at four in the morning," he said. "There won't be another soul on the road."

"Dan, I'm not going to argue with you," I said, laughing. "I'm just telling you what I see."

"What else, then?"

"Were you planning on going to California, too?"

"I *am* going to California. As soon as I finish my business in New York."

"No, you're not," I said. "The five o'clock flight will be canceled."

He checked his mobile phone, which doubled as a datebook. "I don't have a five o'clock flight. I have a noon flight."

"I'm only telling you what I see," I said.

"It makes no sense," he said.

"I'm sorry," I said. "I just tell it as I see it."

He asked a few specific questions about some of the associates he'd be meeting over the course of the trip, and I answered them, but by the end of the reading he seemed a little frustrated. Still, there was nothing to be done about it. Not everything I see is going to make immediate sense—some things only become clear much later, if at all. I've learned not to impose logic on what I see, just as I've learned not to try to interpret details for the client. It's what the client *thinks* it means that really matters. The significance of a dream depends on your interpretation, not on an interpretation imposed on it by outsiders. Dreams are deeply personal. As someone once said, "Dreams tell us things we won't listen to when we're awake."

On Monday, I went to work—an uneventful day—and on Tuesday I went back for more of the same. At two that afternoon, however, I had a text message on my mobile from a girlfriend: "A plane has just crashed into the World Trade Center." She was a bit of a joker, so I scrolled down for the punch line, but there was no punch line. I went into another part of the office and found a group of my colleagues tuned to CNN, openmouthed with horror. A second plane had just struck the neighboring tower. The World Trade Center buildings were falling down as we watched in disbelief.

For the next few days, we all went around in this sort of mute horror. Then, at week's end I had a call from Daniel Moss. He was just back from his trip abroad, and he was calling, breathless with nervous excitement, wanting to review our recent reading. He went through it almost beat by beat: On the way to Heathrow, at four in the morning, there'd been a terrific accident, and he almost missed his flight. In New York, he was staying near the Twin Towers when they collapsed, and he had indeed felt as if the world were coming down around his ears. His son had tried frantically to phone him, to make sure he was safe, but had been unable to get through for several hours. Of course, the scheduled meetings never happened, so the fact that I'd had no distinct "feelings" about the people he was to meet made perfect sense. And of course he didn't go on to California because he wanted to get home to his family. "The first flight out was Friday, at five o'clock. But as you predicted, it was canceled, and I didn't get home till last night."

"What a nightmare," I said, shocked. "Thank God you're okay."

"Lisa," he said. "Everything you told me came true. I will never doubt you again."

Photo by Andrew Thomas

The Hipster

chapter **6**

Meeting the Hipster

I n the weeks following the destruction of the World Trade Center, I found myself busier than ever. I'm not sure what it was, exactly. Perhaps, with everyone still reeling, they were seeking answers, and invariably many of them turned to people like me. I still had a full-time job, but I was also booking about a dozen readings a week.

One reading from this period stands out sharply. There was a woman I'd seen twice already, and on her third visit she brought along her mother. My client was lovely, but her mother was very abrupt. As soon as she entered, she looked me up and down appraisingly. "You're very young, aren't you?" she said without so much as a "hello."

"Excuse me?"

"You're very young to be doing this type of work," she repeated.

"I'm sorry," I said. "I'm twenty-eight and I didn't realize there was an age requirement."

"I'm not saying there is," she said, as she gave me a haughty look. "But you're just a spring chicken. You can't be much good."

"We don't have to do the reading," I said, trying not to show my annoyance.

"No, no," she said. "But I was just telling my daughter, in the car on our way over, about this woman who read for me years ago. She was an older woman, lived on Bartley Green, in Birmingham. I remember going into her house and having to sit on the stairs because she had so many people waiting for her. She's dead now; otherwise I would have gone to her. There was a gentleman there, tending to us—her son, I think. He looked like he enjoyed more than his proper share of drink."

"Mom," my client said. "I think you're being rude."

"I am not," she protested. "I'm entitled to my opinion. I was just telling her about the woman. Her name was Frances. Have you heard of her?"

I paused, pretending to think. "Oh, yes," I said. "I do know her. Would you like a cup of tea?"

I went over to fetch the tea, and on my way back I returned with a photo of my nan. "Is this the Frances you were talking about?" I asked.

"By God, yes. It is! How do you happen to have a picture of her?"

"Because she was my grandmother."

This effectively shut her up, so I continued: "Now, you can continue to insult me further, or we can sit down and listen to what your husband Tom has to say." I indicated the empty chair in the lounge. "He's sitting right there, and he has a lot to tell you."

She couldn't believe it. Her mouth dropped open and she looked from me to the chair and back again.

We proceeded with the reading, and, when we were done, the woman had been converted. "I'd like to book another session," she said.

"I don't have anything for a few months," I said. It was true. I wasn't being coy, my schedule was just crazy.

"If I have to wait, I'll wait," she said. I booked it, half-expecting her to apologize for her rudeness, but the apology never came.

I had another skeptic not two weeks later. "I really don't know why I'm here, but I heard you're quite good," she said. Then, as if to challenge me, she added sternly: "I've waited seven weeks for this appointment."

"I'm sorry," I said. "I have a full-time job, and I like to spend weekends with my son, so I try not to overbook."

"That's fine," she said. "But I'm looking for hard evidence."

"Of what?"

"There's one person in particular I wish to make contact with. I'm not going to tell you who it is, but even if he does show up I'm still going to take some convincing."

As soon as we sat down, a spirit appeared. "Your grandmother's with us," I said.

"Oh?" she said. She looked disappointed.

"She has your father with her," I said.

She perked up, but she looked a little shocked.

"I'm assuming your father passed over?" I said.

"Yes," she said.

"Well, that's a relief," I said. "He's saying something about the tomatoes; how they went everywhere."

"That doesn't mean anything to me," she said.

It didn't mean anything to me, either. "Hold on," I said. "Now he's telling me that you shouldn't have felt badly about the holiday. It wasn't your fault you were away when he passed."

"That was a lucky guess," she said.

"A guess?" I said. "That you were on holiday when he passed?"

"Okay, maybe it's not a guess, but I don't understand what he means about the tomatoes."

I asked him, but he was still going on about the holiday. "He says there was no need to cut it short. He understands that in his heart you said good-bye to him."

"That's rather vague, isn't it? You could say that about anyone. Do you even know what his name is?"

"It's John," I said. "But a lot of people call him Jack."

Now, for most people getting the correct name would have been evidence enough, but not this lady. "Well, that was easy enough," she countered. "John is a common name and most are called Jack, aren't they? I want hard evidence."

By this time even her father was growing irritated, because he offered me an answer. "Tell her I died on your birthday," he said.

"He says he died on your birthday," I said.

"Did not," she replied smugly.

He said it again, and he kept repeating it, until finally he made himself clear. "No," he said. "On *your* birthday."

"I'm sorry," I said. "I got it wrong. It seems he died on my birthday. June nineteenth."

The woman looked completely gone. "I . . . I don't know what to say," she stammered.

"Was that the evidence you needed?"

"Yes," she said.

It's odd, because the session ended shortly thereafter, and she didn't really have many questions for me. It's almost as if she'd only booked an appointment to see if I was the real thing.

Christmas came and went. We spent it with my parents, but on Christmas Day Charlie went over to spend the day with Simon, as planned. I had encouraged Charlie to have a good relationship with his father, as did I. I was a little concerned when I learned he had a rather serious new girlfriend, but I really shouldn't have been. Life moves on. And it's not as if she was going to take my place as Charlie's mother. Also, it made me think of my own life, and how

I needed to get on with it, and in late February of that year, 2002, I discovered a wonder of the modern world—Internet dating. Perfect for a busy, working, single parent, who talked to dead people in her spare time.

I chose the most reputable of the available companies but didn't quite know how to describe myself online. I remember sitting down to write my profile, trying to answer the somewhat laughable questions. *What are you looking for in a man?* I'm just looking for a man, thank you very much. *What do you like to do?* I like to go to bars from time to time, to drink Diet Coke, but if you twist my arm I'll take a real drink. *What do you do for a living?* I'm a witch. *What do you do in your spare time?* I was conscious that I might not get replies if I didn't tick all the right boxes.

As it turned out, I got a lot of responses to my ad, though I'm not sure why. Maybe some of the men thought I had a good sense of humor. I'm sure all of them thought I was joking. They would send e-mails, telling me a little something about themselves, and I would do the same, and when I felt comfortable we would exchange phone numbers and photos. It was odd but amusing. I always got the sense that the guys were trying to figure out if I was good-looking, perhaps thinking that the photo I had sent was not of me. Some of them were painfully shy, some took a lot of interest in me being a single mom, but others were, I'm afraid to say, more direct: "You want to come over and have sex?"

"No, I do not, thank you. What is wrong with you?!"

"Nothing is wrong with me. I want to have sex."

"Don't you want to get to know the person a bit beforehand?"

"Not really. That usually ruins everything."

A lot of the guys wrote detailed profiles that were designed to make them look appealing. Many of them went on about long walks on the beach in the moonlight, and poetry, and I got the impression they'd all read the same book, *Internet Dating for the Complete Idiot*. I thought it was madness to try to make one's self sound appealing.

You didn't really know what people were looking for, so where were you expected to begin? I decided to just say who I was, and to try to let a bit of my personality shine through, and just hope the right person would find me.

I went for coffee with a few guys, and most of them weren't at all who they said they were. Either that or they were seriously delusional. Then I got to chatting with a guy called Lee, and I quite liked the sound of him. We ended up meeting in the middle of the day by a flower stand in the heart of Birmingham. I saw him before he saw me. He was a decent-enough-looking chap, though not at all my type, and he was standing on the corner holding a bouquet of fresh-cut flowers.

I introduced myself, and we went off and had a seat at a coffee shop on Brindley Place. There's a little fountain nearby, and every so often jets of water shoot up into the air, and it's very pleasant to look at. Lee was quite charming, but I wasn't attracted to him, and that made it that much easier to be myself. As a result, we became good friends. I still went for coffee with other guys, and Lee kept trying his luck with other girls, but it was nice to have each other, and we enjoyed reporting back on our respective dating fiascos. "It's rather fun," I told him one day. "I don't think I'm going to meet the man of my dreams anytime soon, but I'm meeting all sorts of nice people, and some of them are quite amusing." There was the occasional psycho in the lot, of course, but that's life.

I met some women on the Internet too. I'd find myself in a chat room, discussing one of my dates with a complete stranger, and then we'd discover that we'd both gone out with the same bloke and started to compare notes. I made some charming girlfriends online, and we had good fun. I remember thinking that that's what the Internet was about: *connecting*.

One evening, I popped over to Lee's and we waited for his brother to turn up before going out for a drink. Lee owned a small recording studio, and his brother was a musician. He showed up at the studio half an hour later with a woman named Kate, who was helping him prepare a few songs for the wedding of a mutual friend. Apparently, they'd only just met, but on the way to the pub I told Lee, "Your brother's going to marry that girl." He laughed it off, but my comment made him curious, and at the end of the evening he asked me to read for him. When we were ready, he asked me straight out, "When am I going to meet The Girl?"

"Not till you're forty," I said.

"Forty," he moaned. "That's another five years. What am I going to do until then?"

"Meet lots of the wrong girls," I said, laughing.

(Not to jump ahead, but I thought you should know that Lee's brother did indeed marry Kate, and I sang at their wedding. Lee himself met a girl on the Internet, on his fortieth birthday, and they were indeed married in March 2007—just as I predicted—and have already had their first baby, a girl—which I'd also predicted.)

Meanwhile, I kept dating. Some of the guys were nice enough, and it was confidence-boosting—they were genuinely interested in little old me, a single mom—but nothing really sparked. Then I met Mike, who sounded charming, but for some odd reason refused to meet me in person. I kept trying to get him to go out with me, but he refused, and his excuses never made any sense. "It's Saturday night," I said. "What's the harm in having a drink with me?"

"I can't," he said. "I have a friend staying with me."

"What's the problem, then? Are you joined at the hip?"

"Not really. Well . . . sort of. I mean, at the moment."

"Wonderful!" I said. "Say hello to the Hipster for me."

Finally, in August 2003, after three months of this nonsense, I wore him down. I told him my friend Jonesy was taking care of Charlie, and that I was free, and that he absolutely *had* to go out with me. Finally, he agreed, so we met at a local bar. I had seen a picture of him, but even so I was not sure what I was expecting. He wasn't my type at all. He was five foot ten, with dark hair, and certainly handsome enough, if you like computer geeky types, but he was wonderful company, as I'd known he would be from our many Internet conversations. We cruised the bars on Broad Street until they closed, and by evening's end I felt as if I'd made a new friend.

"That wasn't so bad now, was it?"

"Torture," he said, but he was grinning.

A couple of weeks went by and one night I was out with Das, another guy I'd met on the Internet, and when I got up to use the bathroom I bumped into Mike and a friend. I knew instantly that he was the Hipster.

"Hi, Mike," I said.

"Hello, Lisa," he said. "Are you here on a date?" He was laughing and trying to peer around the corner to get a look at Das.

"Yes, I am as it happens," I said. I turned to Mike's friend. "You must be the Hipster!"

The Hipster smiled and looked me up and down and said, "Nice to meet you, I'm Kev."

His name was Kevin Harris. He was about six feet tall, with light brown hair and a receding hairline, and he had very nice blue eyes and a charming smile. But he wasn't my type. Actually I had decided I didn't have a type. But no matter. I wasn't really looking for love anymore. I was having fun, and my life was full. We exchanged a few more pleasantries and then went our separate ways.

Two weeks later, however, I was out with a girlfriend, and as we walked to Broad Street from the car park, we passed a shop where they sold all sorts of candles and crystals. We popped in there for a minute, as my friend wanted to get a crystal for her daughter. While my friend was looking at the crystals, I walked over to where they kept the Tarot cards and noticed a young woman sitting on the step flicking through some beautiful cards, and I commented on how pretty they were. She smiled, I could see she was trying to read them, and I had this overwhelming urge to tell her something. I walked around the shop again and went back to her.

"Sorry to bother you. I can see that you are busy, but I have to tell you that everything is going to be okay."

She turned to look at me with tears in her eyes. "You're pregnant, aren't you?" I asked in a whisper so only she could hear.

"Oh my God . . . yes, I am. I found out today. How did you know?"

I told her that I did readings and I just wanted to let her know that she would be fine.

"Oh, and you won't find answers in those cards because you will find it hard to read for yourself," I said, giving her a friendly squeeze on the arm as I turned to walk away. My friend and I were about to leave the shop, when the pregnant girl ran up to me and said, "I want you to have these. They'll be of more use to you than they are to me." She handed me the pack of beautiful cards and I was taken aback, I couldn't believe that someone had been so generous. I had been given a beautiful set of Goddess cards, which I still use to this very day.

After that, my friend and I were enjoying a quiet drink and chatting, when who should walk into the bar but Mike and the Hipster. We had a drink with them, which was pleasant enough, then said our good-byes and went across the street to a different bar. Ten minutes later, just as my Diet Coke arrived, who should walk in but Mike and the Hipster. This was getting familiar. We had another drink together, trying to chat above the noise, and finally moved on separately, but we ran into them again at a third bar.

"Are you following us around, then?" I asked, laughing.

"No, actually we think you're stalking us!" they said cheekily.

We drank and danced and had a great time until last call, at which point we were all in need of food, so in true English tradition, we went off to a curry house and found a quiet table in the corner. I was sitting across from Mike, and my friend was across from Kev.

"Did you know Lisa was a witch?" she said, looking at Kev.

"Excuse me?"

"She's a medium and a clairvoyant."

"Good for her," Kevin said dismissively. I wasn't sure if he believed or not from that remark.

I turned to look at Mike. "You're going to get married within two years, and I'm going to be at your wedding," I said.

"Don't tell me I'm going to marry you!" he protested.

"No. Don't flatter yourself," I said, laughing. "But I'll be there."

"So what do you see happening with me?" Kev asked.

"I see you've been through a bad experience," I said, and I proceeded to describe some of the problems he'd had in a recent relationship.

"I don't want to hear any more," he said abruptly. I could see I had struck a nerve. I felt bad for him, and I offered to read for him if he ever felt so inclined. "I might take you up on that," he said.

I never gave Kev a second thought, but two Fridays later, my mobile rang at one thirty in the morning, waking me. "Hello?" I said.

"Hi, Lisa. It's Kev."

"Kev?"

"Mike's friend. The Hipster."

"Oh, right. How are you?"

"Is it late to be bothering you?" he asked, sounding upset.

"A bit, but don't worry about it. What were you calling about?"

"I was wondering about that reading. I think I'd like to do it."

This was odd, because for some reason he hadn't struck me like the type who needed a reading. "All right," I said. "I'll call you tomorrow to arrange it."

"Do you need my number?"

"No. It came though on my mobile."

"Oh, yes, of course."

I got off the phone and drifted back to sleep, and the next morning I called and was able to squeeze him in for the following Thursday. "I'll be in your neighborhood," I said.

"Maybe it's a sign," he joked, but he seemed a little nervous.

Thursday came and I went to the apartment he shared with Mike. It was an older building, with lots of character, and I remember looking around the flat, thinking how much more they could have done with that beautiful place, but of course two bachelors lived in it, and interior decorating was clearly not a priority.

"Are you ready?" I asked.

"Yes. I think so."

"Do you want to know everything?"

"What does that mean?"

"If I see something bad, do you want to hear it?"

"I guess so. What's the point otherwise?"

I set my little tape recorder on the low table between us, and asked him to give me something personal. He gave me the silver necklace he was wearing, which was quite heavy. I held it in my hand for a few moments, rubbing it between my fingers. "I'm getting the same feeling I got the night I met you," I said. "You've been through a traumatic breakup, and it's been hard, but I can see you coming out of it already. I see you're going on holiday soon, to Thailand or somewhere like that. But when you come back, things are going to be a little different, and I'm getting the name 'Eric.' I don't think you should trust Eric. I think it's connected to your work."

"What do you mean I shouldn't trust Eric?"

"So you know an Eric?"

"Yes. Actually, the only Eric I know is my boss."

"Well, he's the one, then," I said.

"That's crazy," he said, laughing. "Things at work are great. I've just had a promotion." Kev sold computer software to large businesses. He hadn't worked there long, but was really enjoying it.

"Well, I'm sorry," I said. "I don't think you're going to be there long. And afterward, well—you're not going to work for a while. You're going to take some time off, then you'll be offered another position, but instead of taking that job you'll go to work for their competition."

"Are you having me on?" he said, laughing.

"Not at all," I said.

"I don't understand most of it. Leaving. Not working. Working. Going to the competition. It all sounds unbelievable."

"I don't understand it either, but maybe some of it will become clearer when you come back from holiday."

"What else do you see?"

"Does the number 'eighty-nine' mean anything to you?"

"You've got to be kidding," he said, stunned. "Has Mike discussed anything with you?"

"No, honestly. The number means nothing to me."

He got up and crossed the room and came back with some paperwork. He showed it to me. "I have just put a deposit on an apartment being built over by the canals," he said. "The address is 89 Watermarque."

"Maybe it was a lucky guess," I joked.

He sat down again. "What else?"

"Well, I know you may not like this: You're going to marry within a short period of time."

He started laughing and couldn't stop. "Lisa," he finally managed. "I thought you were supposed to be good at this. I was married once, and it was a mistake, and I'm never going through that ordeal again."

"That's what I see," I said.

"Can you see who it is?"

"Well, she's an unmarried mother."

"Oh, yeah!" he said, and started laughing. "Don't get your hopes up, Lisa. You're not my type."

Cheeky sod. "I won't," I said, also laughing. "You're not my type either."

At the end of the evening, he tried to pay me, but I wouldn't take his money. "When it all comes true, you can pay me then," I said.

Three weeks went by before he rang me again. He had just gotten back from, yes, Thailand. "Lisa, I need to see you," he said.

"Back from holiday already?"

"That's what I need to see you about. I came home two days ago, and there's a message from Eric on my machine, telling me I no longer have a job. We've all been made redundant, just as you predicted. You told me not to trust the guy."

"I'm sorry," I said.

"No. Don't be. You know how you said I'd also be taking a few months off? Well, I've made a little money on some property I invested in, so I'm really in no hurry to find work. I've decided to take some time off."

"You're a lucky man," I said. "I wish I could say the same."

We chatted for a while, and I told him that I was unhappy at work, and seriously thinking about moving on.

Kev, always the confident one, said, "You should quit, I know you'll find something better."

"I thought I was the one who saw the future," I said.

"Can't you tell your own future?" he asked.

"If only it were that easy," I said.

Two weeks later, on October 14, I left my job. I didn't have anything else lined up, but to make ends meet I started taking on more clients. I certainly had the time for it.

Then, one morning Kev called to say he was looking for a new job—he'd had enough loafing—and he was wondering if I'd help him with his resumé. I wasn't terribly busy, so I put it together, and he was very appreciative. A few days later he asked me to meet him for lunch. "Please bring the tape recorder; I want to listen to the tape of the reading you gave me," he said.

Charlie was in nursery, and I had no readings till that evening, so I made the half hour drive to Birmingham and met him for pizza. We were sitting in a little café, looking out over the canals and the new developments, and Kev had brought the tape. I slipped it into the recorder and we played it, listening to what I had told him. And I have to say, I sat there listening to the reading with my mouth open. I couldn't believe how accurate I was—I was quite impressed with myself. I'd gotten so much of it right. Then we got to the part about the unmarried mother, and Kev had to laugh. "You blew that one, didn't you?"

I laughed too. I never for a moment thought it might be me.

Still, in the days and weeks ahead, I began to spend a lot of time with Kev. I found I quite liked him, but not in a romantic sense. We'd go shopping, or meet for lunch, and he was very easy to talk to and knew how to treat me like a lady. We became close friends, and I looked forward to our time together, but I never imagined it going any further.

Then one night he called to tell me that his friend Fiona wanted a reading. I told him I was free that Friday—now that I wasn't working, my schedule was fairly open, and Mom had asked if Charlie could stay with her overnight—so Kev said he'd arrange it. He suggested we do the reading at his apartment, and that perhaps we could all go out for a bite to eat after. I'd never been out with Kev at night—he was a daytime friend—but I was looking forward to it. Also, his friend Fiona was going to be there, so I never thought anything else about it.

Friday night he called to tell me that Fiona had chickened out. "She says she's not ready for a reading yet," he said. "But you and I can still go out, right?" He was always confident about himself.

"Sure," I said. "Why not."

I went, and we really had fun. At one point, knowing I didn't have to get back for Charlie, I felt like switching from Diet Coke to a real drink, but I told Kev I'd be no good to drive home.

"You can stay at the apartment. Mike's away," he said, being the perfect gent. "You can sleep on the couch or in his room, if you like."

So I drank. And we had a great time. We'd look around, watching the other people in the bar, checking out the men and women, as I'd done with Lee. I'd point to a guy and say, "What about that one?" And he'd wince and say, "Lisa, you can do much better than that!" And he'd go off to chat up a girl and return with her phone number, and I'd make some crack about his low standards.

We didn't leave till after last orders. I wanted to get a cab, as I had stood all night in three-inch heels, but Kev called me a wuss and told me that we were walking back to his place. I couldn't believe it; it had to be at least a mile away!

I gave in, and started following him back to his apartment, but I whined about the heels, and about being hungry, so we decided to stop for curry and sat across from each other, eating. I found him staring at me.

"You know what, Lisa? If it doesn't happen tonight, I don't think it ever will," he said at last.

"Yeah, right!" I said, laughing a little too nervously for my liking. I couldn't believe he was coming on to me; he was my mate!

After dinner, we continued our walk—the walk that never seemed to end—and when we got to the gate of his building he couldn't find the key to the front gate, nor could he remember the code—typical! It was a big black gate, about six feet high, and he just climbed over it, expecting me to do the same. *He has to be joking,* I thought. *Is this how he shows a girl a good time?* But I climbed the gate anyway, ripping my trousers in the process.

When we were finally in the apartment, I said, "I don't feel comfortable sleeping in Mike's bed, and I'm not sleeping on the sofa—you can!" And the next thing I knew we were kissing and I found myself thinking, *Oh my God! What am I doing? You're not supposed to kiss your best friend!*

After that, we began to spend a lot of time together, but telling absolutely no one. For some reason we didn't want anyone interfering. I would only let him come to my place when Charlie was asleep, because I didn't want them to meet. I didn't think I was ready for that yet.

This went on through December, and suddenly Christmas was around the corner, and one evening I took Charlie to Birmingham to see all the festive lights and decorations. Kev called while we were en route, and when I told him where we were going, he suggested meeting us there. "No," I said. "I'm with Charlie."

And he said, "Lisa, I understand you want to be protective, but we're not just having a relationship—I'm also your friend."

"Okay," I sighed. "We'll be at Brindley Place at six thirty."

We were there at six thirty sharp—I'm a bit of stickler about punctuality, for which I make no apologies. It was right on the canals, everything was lit up beautifully, and it was a clear, crisp night. Suddenly Charlie pointed to a spot behind me, and I turned and saw a man in the distance, moving toward us. He was still so far away that it was a while before I realized it was Kev, but Charlie was fixated, as if he knew the man was coming to see us. Kev arrived right on time and immediately fell to a crouch in front of Charlie's stroller. "Hi, Tiger," he said. "How are you?" Charlie lit up and laughed, then looked over at me and smiled. He liked this man. The bond was instant and inexplicable. The three us went off to look at the lights on Broad Street, then went to a restaurant for a bite to eat.

"I just want fries," Charlie said as soon as we were seated.

"No," I said. "They only have pizza. They don't serve fries here. You'll have to have a cheese pizza."

"No, I just want fries!" Charlie takes after his mom, being very fussy with his eating.

"Right, if he wants fries, we'll get him fries."

"Okay," I said, pleasantly surprised by Kev's understanding, especially as he had never had children of his own.

So we left and went up the street to a place that served fries, the waitress brought Charlie some crayons, and he and Kev sat next to each other, drawing away. "Er . . . hello!" I said. "I'm over here. Does anyone know I exist?" But I didn't mean it. I was thrilled, actually, watching the two of them. They looked like they belonged together.

As we were leaving the restaurant, we ran into a woman whom I'd read for in the past, and she hurried over. "Lisa, I need another reading, but I don't want to wait three months!" she said.

"It's not three months anymore," I said. "I'm not working now. I can probably squeeze you in next week or the week after. Call me."

"Okay, I will," she said, and I turned back to Kev and Charlie.

"You have a three-month waiting list to do readings?" Kev asked.

"I did when I was working," I said. "It's a little shorter now. I'm just not very good about scheduling things; my diary's all over the place."

"I don't understand why you're looking for another job," he said. "In my opinion, you could do this full-time."

"You really think so?" I said.

"Absolutely," he said. "You're bloody good at it. You helped me when I needed it and I'm convinced you can do the same for others. Besides, I will always give you the support you need, so don't worry."

I thought about that a moment, and was pleased. The man was right. He knew it and so did I.

Photo by Kevin Harris

*Leaving milk and cookies for Santa on
Christmas Eve with Mike and Jonesy*

chapter 7

A New Start

When Christmas rolled around, Charlie and I went to my parents' for the traditional Christmas lunch. I didn't invite Kev because I hadn't introduced him to my family yet, and he had family obligations of his own. I remember I wasn't feeling at all well when we arrived, and both Charlie and Kev had colds, so I assumed I was coming down with a cold of my own. I looked over at Charlie, sitting directly across the table from me, and eating like a perfect gentleman. He was going to his dad's the following day, Boxing Day, and I was missing him already.

In the middle of lunch, feeling suddenly horrible, I excused myself and went to the guest room to lie down, but it only made it worse. My mom came in and took one look at me and said I didn't look well at all. "I feel awful," I said. "I think I'm going to take Charlie home."

We got back to the house and Charlie took out his toys and began to play. I lay nearby, on the sofa, feeling increasingly ill. I felt very hot, and I asked Ben or anyone else in the spirit world to please send me some healing. I was seldom sick, and I'd certainly never felt as sick as I felt then. I began to feel intense pain in my stomach, and it kept getting worse.

By nine o'clock the pain was so bad that I was having trouble breathing, but I managed to put Charlie to bed and decided to call a doctor. I dialed the National Health Service—they have a 24-hour phone line, NHS-Direct—and they said a doctor would be calling back shortly. I took some painkillers—a rarity for me—then lay in bed with the hot-water bottle on my stomach, waiting for the call that never came. I woke at five in the morning in excruciating pain. It was too early to call Mom or anyone else, so I tried NHS-Direct again. "We'll have a doctor call you back shortly," the woman said.

"That's what you said last night," I told her. "I am in horrific pain. I need to know what this is *now*."

"Yes, ma'am. I understand."

I hung up, and Charlie came padding into the room. He climbed on the bed and immediately started stroking my belly. "It's okay, Mummy," he said. "It's okay." Then he reached for the phone and handed it to me. "Phone Nanny," he said. "Phone Nanny to come." I was flabbergasted. How did my two-and-a-half-year-old son know that I needed help? To see me in pain was one thing, but to urge me to call my mother was something else entirely. I dialed my parents' number and my mother picked up. "Mom," I said, "you're going to have to come get Charlie, and Dad's going to have to take me to the hospital."

"Okay," she said, trying to keep the worry out of her voice. "I'll be there in fifteen minutes."

She knew something was wrong, because I'm seldom ill and I have a high tolerance for pain, and when she and Dad arrived I could see the terror in their eyes. "I'll be all right," I said, but I didn't feel all right at all.

By the time we got to primary care, I was doubled over in pain. It felt like one long, interminable contraction, multiplied by ten.

The admitting nurse gave us some forms to fill out and Dad asked me questions and did what he could, but by this time it felt as if my insides were about to burst. My father, seeing this, became hugely irate, and he went off to confront the nurse at the admitting desk. "Listen here! Most of these people have coughs and colds. My daughter is obviously very ill. She needs a doctor right now!"

I'd never seen my father like that, but it worked. The nurse took my pulse, which was at 115, then put me in a wheelchair and rushed me into the ward. A doctor came to see me a few minutes later, and he studied the form, mumbling to himself: "History of cancer. Hmm. Interesting." He hadn't even looked at me or at my stomach, which by now felt like a raging volcano. I began screaming in agony, and a second doctor appeared and quickly sedated me. When I woke up, probably hours later, I was hooked up to an IV and to all manner of bleating, bleeping monitors. The second doctor returned and told me that I had a severe infection in my fallopian tubes, and that I was being treated with megadoses of intravenous antibiotics. I would be there for at least three days, he said.

I nodded off again, and when I woke up I found my bag and dug around for my mobile. There was a text message from Kev, saying hello and sending his love. I texted back that I was in the hospital, and that we'd talk later. He didn't respond.

A few hours later, I woke from another nap, and when I opened my eyes Kev was walking into the room. "What's going on, then?" he said, smiling broadly.

"Aren't you supposed to be with your family?"

"This was the excuse I need to get away," he said.

I was really pleased to see Kev. I didn't really know where the relationship was going, or even where I wanted it to go, but this little gesture said a great deal about him—all of it good.

I was in the hospital for five days, but it was Christmastime, so there were only a few appointments to cancel, and when I got home I actually had a few days of complete rest.

As the New Year got underway, with my health suddenly much improved, my new career began to take off. Kev had a good business head on his shoulders and from time to time helped me organize myself in a more professional way. I remember driving out to Staples to buy my first appointments diary, and when I got home I started phoning clients to tell them I was now free during the day. I didn't think anyone would want a reading during the day, but Kev had insisted that I had to take control of my diary and he was right. By the end of January, I was booking twenty readings a week, and new clients were calling every day. The year 2003 was off to a promising start.

That very first week, I had a new client who informed me right away that her mother had been murdered. "I want to know what happened, and whether the right person is in jail for it," she said. She was just a child when her mother was killed, and all these years later she still had doubts about the crime. "If you can give me the name of the man who did it, then I'll know," she said.

I asked her if she wanted to know everything and she said she did. Her mother came through straightaway, and told her daughter that she was proud of her and that she was not to worry, as her passing didn't hurt and she was protecting her throughout life. I asked her if she could give me the name of the person who killed her. Straightaway a name was shouted out to me. Not like you hear someone talking to you out loud, but it was like someone was shouting deep inside my head.

"I'm hearing the name 'Robert,'" I said. She went absolutely white, and for a moment I thought she was going to be sick. "Are you all right?" I asked.

She nodded, then took a deep breath. "There was always doubt in my mind because I didn't want to believe it, and because he's been denying it these many years, but now I know it's him. Now I know it was my dad who killed her."

I felt awful for her. All these years she had wanted to believe her father was innocent, and I'd taken that from her. "I'm sorry," I said.

"No," she said. "We only believe certain things because we want to believe them, but it was time to let go. I had to face the truth. Thank you. I will always be grateful for this."

After she left, I couldn't get her out of my mind. I still felt as if I had taken something away from her. It may have well been an illusion, but some of us need our illusions to get out of bed in the morning. I was really on the fence about it. For a long time I wondered if I'd had the right to tell what I saw and heard, to her or to anyone else, and I was very conflicted. Then it dawned on me that it wasn't up to me to decide. Who was I to judge whether one of my revelations helped or harmed a client? And if I kept something from them, wasn't that a form of lying? I thought back to some of my earlier readings. I felt I had never been less than honest in my work, though there was one occasion when I decided I couldn't tell the client everything, until she asked the question. An old woman had come in for a reading, and the moment she sat down her husband in spirit said, "I am waiting for her." I knew immediately that she was going to pass over soon. I decided that I was not going to share that with her, but toward the end of the reading, I asked if she had any questions and she said, "When am I going to die?"

Whoa . . . I couldn't believe that she had asked that, but I was honest and I told her, "Your husband told me that he is waiting for you." She smiled and said thank you, paid me, and left. I thought back on the reading and wondered if I'd had a valid reason for not initially telling her. I realized it was not my information to hold back and decided that the spirits will only tell people what they need to know and what they can cope with. So I decided that from that day forth I would never be anything but completely truthful with my clients. As I said, I didn't have the right to decide, and it wasn't me telling them these things. It was the spirits. It occurred to me that they made all the decisions about what they wanted to share, and that there was probably plenty of information they kept to themselves.

With the phone ringing off the hook and my appointments diary filling up quickly, I thought back to what my grandmother had told me: *You will continue my work.* She'd been spot on. That made me think back to some of her other predictions: She'd said I'd make a name for myself in America, which seemed odd, since I didn't know a soul there, and she said there would be two older men in my life. I wondered if Kev was one of them. He was eleven years older than me, though until then I'd never really thought of him as *older.* The other older man remained a mystery.

That summer, six months into my relationship with Kev, I finally introduced him to my family. I didn't know why I was hiding

Photo by Kevin Harris

Our first holiday snap!

him. I was crazy about the guy, and so was Charlie. We were seeing each other three or four nights a week, and he had become an
integral part of my work life too. I wasn't much good at organizing
my appointments diary, and one day Kevin simply took over. Every
morning, he'd lay out my day for me. "You have a ten o'clock with
Molly, at the house, a noon reading with Kathy, and Raj is coming
around at five."

"Five o'clock—isn't that a bit late for Raj?"

"You're the one they're coming to see," he said. "And you have
a life too. Don't be so accommodating. Let them work around your
schedule, not vice versa."

I had a little trouble with that. In those days, I didn't see what
I was doing as a job. I was just trying to help people, and I jumped
through hoops to make myself available. If I had some talent in this
area, however limited it might be, I felt it was my responsibility to
use it to help people. Kevin didn't disagree, but he was right about
the importance of living my own life. "Therapists help people too,"
he said. "But their clients show up when they're told to show up.
And the same with doctors, except you have to wait three months
to see them, even if you're dying."

It made perfect sense. As Kev put it, I was running a business,
and I should treat it as such. "You have a talent for this," he said.
"Some people have a talent for painting or writing or architecture,
and they get paid for it. Why is this any different?"

"I don't know," I said. "Sometimes I'm not convinced I'm all
that good at it."

"Not good at it? You've got women calling round asking you to
teach them how to do what you do."

It was true. Among my clients, there were three or four who
had been begging me to teach them to do what I did, but I resisted
because I wasn't sure it was something one could learn. It was also
true that I sometimes doubted my own talents. This isn't false mod-
esty, either. The truth is, I'd always been a little insecure. I was never

the prettiest girl, never the smartest, never the most popular. You tend to carry those feelings into adulthood.

Now Kev was urging me to be more confident, to see myself as he and others saw me, and it was quite liberating. Two months after that conversation, three women were gathered at my place for Lesson #1. "The first thing I'm going to tell you is that not everything you're going to see and feel makes sense," I said. "In fact, most of it *doesn't* make sense. You'll try to work it out and everything looks pear-shaped, because the rules of logic don't apply. Don't worry about logic. Your job is to tell the client what you see, and to look for detail while you're at it. No detail is too small. A single red rose on a bed may mean nothing to you, but to the client it might unlock a mystery."

I taught them about Tarot Cards (past, present, future), Psycards, and Goddess cards. I covered the basics of psychometry, passing personal items back and forth and trying to pick up "vibes." And I hammered away at them about the need for honesty. "At the beginning of every session, you should ask the client if they want to know everything," I said. "If they don't, then use your discretion, but personally I still tell them what I see, I just word it in a different way. If they want to know everything, you can't hold back. You can't filter. You can't decide what to share and what to leave out. You don't have that right. You're not in charge. The spirits are."

To make real headway, I said, they had to work on themselves, too. We talked about the fact that most people tend to dwell on the past, which I'd been guilty of myself, but noted that life was about *forward movement,* and stressed the importance of letting history go. "It pays to understand the forces that shaped you," I said, "but it doesn't pay to hold on to them."

To illustrate, I told them about a client who'd been to see me some months earlier. She had brought a friend along, and the two women had no sooner stepped through the door when I turned to the friend and said, "Your father says he's sorry." The poor woman started sobbing, and it took her a while to pull herself together. I didn't ask what her father was apologizing for, because it wasn't my business, and in all frankness I didn't want to know, but I could see that she had been holding on to it her whole life, and on that afternoon she took her first step toward letting go. Some weeks later, she came to see me for a reading of her own, and she told me I had transformed her life—that she'd been liberated though forgiveness. But I believe that long before she met me she had the power to let go of the anger and the hurt.

"Nothing quite clutters the mind like the past," I told my students. It is tough on all of us, but it is doubly tough on anyone who hopes to open up his or her mind to worlds beyond the earthly plane. A cluttered mind is a noisy mind, but a clear mind is a *listening* mind—and the spirits are attracted to listeners.

I also spoke to my students about dreams, and how the very vivid ones might not be dreams at all, but visitations. A sleeping mind is less cluttered, and hence more open to possibilities we don't fully comprehend. "A dream might open the door to things you won't face when you're awake," I said.

Similarly, I talked about tricks of memory, how sometimes we remember things that we know couldn't possibly have happened. These memories don't seem to be our own, and it's more than possible that they're *not* our own. They could be a fragment of something we read in a book years ago, for example, a story we were told when we were very small, or something we saw in a long-ago film. But some of them are most definitely connected to past lives.

I wholeheartedly believe in reincarnation. I believe we die and are reborn in an endless cycle of learning, and that we end up in a place that is beyond our understanding, beyond even the power or our imagination, but only when all lessons have been learned.

Some people have been born many times, and they are clearly further along the evolutionary scale than others. These are the "old souls" who have passed this way before. The more gifted ones tend to leave an imprint. Musicians, actors, writers, humanitarians. All people are created equal, but perhaps we evolve at different rates—over many lifetimes.

I even told my students a little story about my son, Charlie. When he was barely three years old, we were curled up in my bed together, and he said, "You know something, Mummy, before I came, God told me that I had to be born to look after you."

I looked at him, surprised. "Oh, he did, did he?"

"Yes. He knew that you and Daddy weren't going to be together, and he thought it would be nice for us to be together, so I could look after you, and that's why I'm here."

I had to fight the tears. "And I'm very glad you are," I said.

"Me too," he said.

I'd like to think my students learned a thing or two from me, and I know that I learned a great deal from teaching them. (One of my students, Margaret, went on to read for the clients I left behind when I eventually moved to the United States, and I am very proud of her. She has read for me on several occasions, so I know how good she has become.) Teaching reinforced some of the things I already knew—the need for honesty, for example, and the importance of detail—and it made me more aware of my own gifts. I really *was* good at this. I really *did* have a gift. The goal now would be to keep evolving further along the spiritual pathway. At the same time, I realized that the gift was unquantifiable. You couldn't measure these talents, which wasn't the point, anyway. It wasn't about being *good,* or about being the best, it was about *always working to improve,* on all levels, and *utilizing my gift to educate and benefit others.*

And I believe I did get better. I became more attuned to the spirits, and, in doing so, a little more worried, too. Sometimes, long after a client had gone home, the spirits would remain behind. I'd be watching TV, say, and I'd feel a spirit sitting next to me. Or I'd be in the bath, and I'd sense the spirit watching. It wasn't frightening, exactly, but it was certainly discomfiting. I didn't want to bring any negativity into the house. I had Charlie to think about. I knew my grandfather would protect him—I often sensed his presence when I went into Charlie's room—but I didn't want to take any risks.

"I was thinking it might be nice to do the readings outside the house," I told Kevin one night over dinner. "I'd like to keep the business and my personal life separate."

The trick was finding something I could afford.

For the next week or two, I halfheartedly looked through the classifieds, hoping I'd stumble across the perfect little place, but nothing jumped at me. Then one night I had a woman over for a reading and the experience snapped me out of my lethargy. We were downstairs, in mid-session. Charlie was fast asleep in bed. I felt a little chill in the room, and looked around, but I didn't see anything.

"What is it?" the client asked.

"I'm not sure," I said. "I feel a lot of negative energy in the room."

At that moment, I heard Charlie's electric guitar going off—a crazy, screeching riff unlike anything I'd ever heard before—and I bolted to my feet, my heart pounding like crazy. "Oh my God!" I said. "Did you hear that?"

"Of course I heard it!" my client said.

I raced upstairs, my heart still beating crazily—*ka-thump, ka-thump, ka-thump*—and burst into Charlie's room. Charlie was fast asleep, and the guitar was lying at the foot of his bed, face down. It was still humming faintly, but when the sound faded I could only hear my wildly pumping heart. I couldn't understand how the guitar had gotten there, because I'd put it away before tucking him in—I remembered that distinctly. I walked over to the bed and looked down at Charlie. He was breathing peacefully. He looked happy. I went over and picked up the guitar, tentatively, and carried it out into the corridor. I left it there and rejoined my client.

"Is everything all right?" she asked.

"Yes," I said. I was a little freaked out. It was one thing to have a conversation with a dead person, but this had felt distinctly negative, and at the time I felt it was out of my league. I finished the reading, but I was still concerned about the lingering negativity. I showed my client to the door and hurried upstairs to look in on Charlie. I picked him up and took him to my bed, and I didn't take my hand off him all night.

In the morning, I called Kev to tell him what had happened, and to urge him to help me find a place for my readings. After I dropped Charlie at nursery, I went to the library to see what I could find on evil spirits. The book I liked best was *The Art of Psychic Protection* by Judy Hall, a psychic and healer. The moment I finished reading it, I rushed out to get everything I needed to make the house safe from evil spirits. I bought crystals that detracted negative energy and placed them in the windows. And I put dried sage in every nook and cranny. The smell of the sage was so pungent that people would come in and wonder if I'd been smoking something funny.

That night, after I was done evil-proofing the house, Ben, my spirit guide, made a rare appearance. "Where have you been?" I said. "I haven't seen you in months and months."

"I don't want you to worry about Charlie," he said. "I'll always keep an eye on him."

And with that, he was gone. In the morning I wondered whether I had simply dreamed him, to make myself feel safe. I hoped not, because I appreciated his help, but it was hard to tell. He was an elusive bugger.

One of my more memorable readings from this period concerned a very businesslike lady, with long, auburn hair, who, like most of my clients, was referred to me through friends. I made her a cup of tea, sat her down, and asked her for a personal item. She gave me her watch and I switched on my tape recorder. "I have someone here who is baking muffins," I said. "Either muffins or fairy cakes, I can't quite see."

Immediately, the lady started to cry, and a moment later I said in a girlish voice, "Don't cry, mummy!" She looked up at me, startled, and dabbed at her tears. "I'm sorry," I said. "I don't know why it came out that way."

"No, please. Go on. That's my daughter, Lucy."

"I'm sorry," I said. I had no idea she'd lost a child, and, having a child of my own, I could only imagine how life-alteringly devastating that might be. She made a little gesture for me to go on, and I looked toward the image. The little girl was just off to my right, standing there smiling, tending to her baking. "Ask her about Jenny," the little girl said.

"She said to ask you about Jenny."

The lady had finished dabbing at her tears, and she crumpled the moist tissue into her hand. "That's very strange," she said. "About a year ago, maybe a year and a half ago, you read for a lady called Jenny. You told her that she would be hearing about a little girl who would die. That was Lucy. She was my little girl."

"Jenny is the friend who recommended you?"

"No. I don't know Jenny. But I have a friend who knows her, and she told her about you, and that's how I came to be here. I'm still trying to get my head around the idea that you spoke to someone I didn't know and were able to see my daughter's fatal accident a year before it happened."

"I don't understand it either," I said. "But I've learned not to try. If there are rules in the spirit world, I'm not sure any of us are really able to decipher them."

"Can you see what happened to her?"

"To your daughter?"

"Yes."

I turned to look. Lucy was riding a bike now. I watched as her foot slipped and she crashed into the curb and sailed over the handlebars. One of the handlebars struck her in the belly with great force. I reported this to Lucy's mother. She began to cry again, nodding. "The doctors said she'd done irreparable damage to her liver," she said.

"But it wasn't your fault, Mummy!" Lucy said.

"She says it wasn't your fault."

"I know. In my heart I know, but I'm not there yet. Guilt is a terrible thing."

"But you know it wasn't your fault," I said. "And she knows."

Suddenly Lucy piped up again. "You need to take care of your ovaries."

"She says you need to take care of your ovaries," I said.

"My ovaries? I have no ovaries. I had a hysterectomy a few years ago."

I turned back to ask Lucy for clarification, but she was gone. "Maybe she didn't mean ovaries," the lady suggested. "She's just a little girl. She doesn't know what an ovary is."

"Perhaps you're right. Perhaps she's warning you about something else. But my advice is to keep an eye on your overall health."

After she was gone, I worried that maybe I'd got my signals crossed, which happened from time to time, and that maybe Lucy had been trying to warn me. I'd already had a heap of trouble in that department, so it seemed like a distinct possibility. But nine months later the woman came back for another reading. "Lisa, do you remember what you told me about my ovaries?" she said.

"No," I said. I don't always recall details from previous readings. "Would you refresh my memory?"

"Well, as I told you at the time, I thought my ovaries had been removed, but shortly after the reading I went to see my regular doctor about a terrible pain. Not only did I still have an ovary, there was a tumor in it, and it was cancerous. When we talked to the doctor who performed the operation about it, he said he'd left one of them inside thinking it would balance my hormones. I still can't believe you knew that; it's incredible!"

Even though I have been doing this for years I am still amazed at what I am able to tell people. We continued with our reading, and Lucy appeared, although only briefly. "Tell her I'm coming back."

"What?" I said.

"Tell her I'm coming back."

The lady looked at me. "Is that Lucy?"

"Yep," I said. "She said to tell you she is coming back."

We both got chills. We had no idea what it meant, but of course the story didn't end there. A year later the woman came back, once again determined to speak to Lucy. But Lucy was nowhere to be found. "I don't know how to explain this to you, but I'm getting a distinct feeling that she's no longer in the spirit world," I said. "It's just a feeling, but I think she has gone."

"How do you mean 'gone'?" she asked.

"I don't know," I said. "I can't explain it."

The lady shook her head from side to side, as if this was too much to bear, and after a silence she said: "This is all very strange. I actually came here today to tell Lucy that I was about to adopt another child. The child was born earlier this week, and if I'm going to move forward, this is my only chance. I think I was here to ask Lucy for her blessing."

I could feel the hair standing up on the back of my neck. I didn't understand what the hell was going on, but I remembered what Lucy had said a year earlier: *Tell her I'm coming back.*

That night, I told Kev the story. "What are you saying, then? That she's been reincarnated as this baby the lady's going to adopt?"

"I'm not sure. I guess I'm saying it's possible."

"So you believe in reincarnation?"

"I do, yes. I believe what the Buddhists believe, that we keep being reborn until we get it right. And that it's all connected to karma: If you're good in this life, you'll be rewarded in the next."

"And if you're bad," Kev said, grinning, "you'll come back as a dog."

The following week, Kev was offered a job selling software, and he went in to meet with the team. They liked each other and he was quick to accept their offer, but the day before he was expected to report for work he received a call from a rival company and went to work for them instead. He came over that night in a daze. "That's exactly what you predicted," he said.

Even with the new job, Kev continued to handle my appointments diary, and we settled into a pleasant, homey routine. My life was great on every level: Charlie, Kev, work. Oddly enough, during this period of domestic bliss, I found myself reading for a string of women who were having serious trouble with their mates. I remember telling one of them that her husband was cheating on her, and I provided a few telling details, including the name of the place her husband had been frequenting with his lover. The name of the young woman eluded me, but my client stormed home with enough detail to confront her husband.

The next day, at six in the evening, there's a sudden pounding on my front door. I opened up to find a very angry man standing outside, his nostrils flaring, but he was on the small side, so I wasn't intimidated. "Are you Lisa Williams?!" he bellowed.

"I am."

"How dare you tell my wife I'm cheating on her? What right do you have? It's a load of bullshit."

"I—"

"She's taken the children and she's leaving me! I hope you're proud of yourself, ruining the life of an innocent man!"

I composed myself. "The question is, are you proud of yourself, because it's quite obvious to me you're having an affair with Tracy."

His jaw dropped and the fight went out of him in a flash. I was a little shocked myself, to be honest. I don't know *how* the woman's name came to me, but it was obvious I had it right, thankfully.

"W-who are you?" he stammered. "How do you know about Tracy?"

"This is my job. This is what I do."

Then, to my surprise, he asked, "How do I get an appointment with you?"

"Call this number and schedule it," I said as I handed him my card and closed the door.

In early June 2003, two weeks before my thirtieth birthday, I got a call that I was certain was a hoax. A man called from London claiming to be a hugely successful entertainer. Not knowing quite what to say, I simply played along. "Yes," I said. "This is Lisa Williams. What can I do for you?"

He went on to tell me that he had heard about me through a friend of a friend, and then, that same week someone else had mentioned my name to him. "I don't believe in coincidences, so I'm calling you for a reading," the entertainer said.

I was curious about who these people were, but I didn't prod him for details. "I don't believe in coincidences either," I said.

"Good," he said. "Now here's the situation: I'm leaving for LA shortly, and I'll be gone for a long stretch, and I was hoping you'd be free on the eighteenth. I live in Chelsea, but I'll be glad to send a driver for you."

"What? All the way to Redditch?" I said. "That's a bit much. I'll just catch the train, and perhaps you can have someone meet me at Euston Station."

"Done," he said.

I immediately called Kev. "You'll never believe who I was just on the phone with."

"Who?" he said.

I told him, and he was very impressed. When I gave him the date, Kev said he had business in London that day, and that he'd meet me at the station. "I don't want you to go alone," he said.

On June 18, 2003, the day before my thirtieth birthday I took the train to London and met Kev at the station. The driver was just outside, as promised, holding up a little sign with my name on it. It made me feel rather important. He walked us out to a shiny black Mercedes and drove us to a lovely apartment building in Chelsea, just off King's Road. When I rang the bell, the entertainer came to the door himself. He was ever so charming, and made us feel totally at home, even making a cup of tea for Kev.

He introduced us to his massive dog, and after finishing his tea, Kev said his polite good-byes and headed to the door. "I'll call you when I'm done," I said.

The reading got underway, and the entertainer had very specific questions, some of them business related, but most of them related to a number of projects he was involved with at the time, and some of the people he'd be working with. I shared the feelings I was getting, spoke to him about the spirits that had joined us and what they had to say. Two hours later the reading was over, and he seemed very pleased. I called Kev and he came to meet me. "Keep in touch," my client said to us both. "I have a feeling you and I are going to be friends for a long time."

I guess he must be a little psychic himself, because we are friends to this day.

Kev and I both got into the car and the driver took us all the way back to Redditch.

The next day we began to celebrate my birthday. I say *began* because the celebrations lasted for five days. Janey had organized lunch with the girls, then I had dinner with Kev, followed by a series of lunches with friends, festive dinners, nights clubbing, and finally a big bash at Janey's house. At one point, Janey made a toast: "Lisa's thirty now, and I think it's high time she grew up and stopped drinking Diet Coke." There was a burst of applause, and plenty of hooting and hollering, and a moment later I heard the loud *pop* of a champagne cork. I had a glass or two of the bubbly to celebrate my new maturity, and I had a feeling—though not one of *those* feelings—that I might grow to like the stuff.

Kev was with me for the entire five-day celebration, and it marked a real turning point in our relationship. Not long after the party, I mentioned that I was looking for a bigger house, and he asked me how I felt about buying. "Oh, I'm not ready for that yet," I said. "Financially or otherwise. I prefer renting." He said he'd been looking to invest in another property, and wondered how I would feel about renting from him. "It'll work to my benefit too," he said. "I won't have to look around for a tenant." I thought it might be a little strange, having my boyfriend as a landlord, but Kev assured me I had nothing to worry about, and we immediately began house hunting. In no time at all, we found a charming Victoria cottage dating back to 1845. It had a wonderful little room at the front of the house, which would serve perfectly as a place to give my readings, a nice-size lounge, a kitchen in need of repair, and two bedrooms upstairs. We fell in love with the place on the spot. It needed work, but Kev liked a project, and he was delighted to take this one on.

Charlie and I moved in on August 1, 2003. Straight off, the house felt like a real home. It was cozy, and warm-feeling, with a working fireplace and a long, narrow garden out back. Kev thought it was pretty homey too, because before long he had practically moved in. I went out and bought him a toothbrush, which was a sound investment: The man was worth it.

To some of our friends, it seemed a bit odd that Kev was still sharing the flat on Watermarque with Mike, and that I was paying him rent, but we were both very happy with the arrangement, and that's what counted. I always paid the rent on time, and I knew I could rely on my landlord to rush over at a moment's notice to fix any little thing that went wrong. And sometimes he cooked dinner and spent the night. How great is that?!

At that point, I was doing up to four readings a day, either face to face with the client or over the telephone, five days a week, and sometimes two or three readings on weekends. I also had regular chats with my celebrity friend, who would call from his second home in Los Angeles.

I was also branching out into new, related areas. One of my clients, for example, was a Reiki master, and when I expressed interest in learning more, she offered to take me though my first attunement. I wasn't sure what that meant exactly, but she explained it when she arrived at my house a few days later. She had brought flowers and bells and little items she described as Reiki symbols. "This simple ceremony will teach you how to tune your energies to the Universal Life Force," she said. "That's the first step toward becoming a practitioner of this healing art."

I sat on a stool with my hands clasped in prayer while she danced, waved the symbols and rang her bell around my head, chanted, and circled me more times than I could count. I must admit, I found the whole thing amusing and a bit silly. I had to fight the urge to laugh at first, but I took it seriously nonetheless, and for the next three weeks I followed her directions for self-healing. The idea was to connect with the natural healing qualities that surround us all, and to try to channel them through my hands, and into my body. It sounded a bit strange, but it turned out to be an incredibly powerful experience, and I found myself going through a real roller coaster of emotions. It was actually quite astonishing. I could literally feel the energy in the air, and I would put a hand on a certain part of my body and become somehow cleansed. There were times when it felt as if my hands were magnetized, literally pulling impurities out of my body. I was intrigued and eager to find out more.

As fate would have it, some months later I had two brief experiences, back to back, that made me plunge back in. The first involved a new client, a woman I had never met, who arrived for her first reading looking very depressed indeed. She looked so weighed down with emotional baggage that I suggested we do a healing instead of a reading. I don't know where I got the confidence to suggest such a thing, but I suspect the spirits were pushing me along.

"What would that involve?" she asked.

"I'll just start by putting my hands on your shoulders," I said. "And we'll go from there."

I stood behind her chair and gently placed my hands on her shoulders, and in a matter of seconds they felt strangely hot. I found that I couldn't move my hands, as if they were glued to her, and I could feel her whole body relax. Suddenly I felt light and free. I asked permission from the spirits to remove my hands and it wasn't until they gave me consent that I was able to move them. She turned her head round to look at me, and she was grinning—transformed. "I don't know what you just did," she said. "But I feel lighter than I've felt in years!"

I didn't know what I'd done either, and I was a little startled myself. But I just smiled and said, "Glad I could be of help."

I felt energized, as if I could heal the world.

The second experience took place one Saturday at the home of a girlfriend, Anne. She was moving house and I went over to help her pack. While we were working away, her mother arrived, and I went over to greet her. "Hi, Sally," I said. "How are you?" As I said this, I reached up and put my hand to her face, cupping it against her left jaw. I have no idea why I did this—we knew each other, but not that well—and I immediately removed my hand, feeling somewhat embarrassed.

"Fine," she said, smiling awkwardly. "Thanks for asking."

She then left to fetch some boxes, and I had to run off to pick up Charlie, so I was gone before she returned.

Three weeks later, I was at my friend's house when her mother came in and seemed excited to see me. "Lisa," she said. "Do you remember the other Saturday, when you were helping Anne move?"

"Of course, and I have to say I'm sorry for putting my hand on your face. I've been thinking about that ever since, and I feel a little embarrassed about it," I said.

"Well, don't be, because the strangest thing happened. At the time I had the most severe toothache, and my dentist couldn't see me until the following Tuesday, but you placed your hand on my face and later I realized that the pain was gone."

My own life, thankfully, was pain-free. And getting more pleasant every day: By October, Kev was practically living with Charlie and me. One unseasonably chilly night he came over for dinner and put up a nice fire in the fireplace. Afterward, he helped me wash up, then sat down to play with Charlie. I dropped onto the sofa with a book—I love thrillers—and looked up at them. I thought I'd never seen such a perfect picture of domesticity. When they were done, I put Charlie to bed, and I came downstairs and told Kev I was going to give him a proper reading.

"Why?" he asked.

"I don't really know, but I just feel I need to."

"Okay."

"But I'm going to read for you as I would for any of my regular clients. I'm taking off my Lisa head and I'm going to put my witchy head on."

"Fine with me," he said.

We got started. "You're going away," I said. "I don't know where you're going, but it'll be an offer you can't refuse. I also see you're going to have a problem with your visa, so check your papers."

"Am I going overseas, then?"

"I think so, but I am not sure where. You'll be going with a woman, who will have a near-death experience."

"Something to look forward to," he joked. Then turning serious, "Is it you?"

I ignored him. "I also get the feeling that you're not going to be working much longer. Not in your current job, anyway. I see you becoming more of a manager."

"Manager? Of what?"

"I'm not sure," I said. "Me, maybe."

"Well, your schedule could use a little streamlining," he said. "Maybe that's what you're talking about."

"Come on," I said. "I'm being serious here. I see you're going to move into a place of your own, and that you'll marry, and that you'll take responsibility for two children."

"But you've only got one," he said.

"I didn't say I was talking about me," I said.

"So you're saying I might actually marry again, but not to you?"

I looked up at him, exasperated. "How many times do I have to tell you? I don't always understand what I see."

I gave up on the reading, and went off to "cook some tea," as we like to say in England, and when we were done we went to bed. "You do know I won't marry again, don't you?" he said, reaching for my hand.

"Yes," I said.

"So why do you keep telling me I'll marry again? You told me that at my very first reading, and you're telling me again tonight."

"Kev, I just tell you what I'm given. I don't try to make sense of it."

The following week, my entertainer friend called from Los Angeles. When the reading was over, he said, "You know, Lisa, you need to come to LA."

"Why do you say that?"

"I'm telling you, you will absolutely love it here, and LA is going to love you. You've got to make it happen."

"Maybe I'll talk to Kev," I said. "We could come for a couple of weeks."

"No, that would never work," he said. "If you come, and I'm urging you to come, it's got to be for at least three months."

When Kev came over that night, I told him about the conversation, and he seemed quite enthused. He thought three months was a bit much, but said we might manage a month. When I next spoke to my friend, he refused to hear it. "Listen," he said. "You need at least three months here. I promise you, you will fall in love with the place. And it will fall in love with you. But stop waffling. The next time I speak to you, I want to hear that you're committing to three months."

Kev and I talked about it again, and he decided it might be worth a try. He had been thinking of taking a one-month leave of absence from his job, which didn't seem to be going anywhere, but now he decided it might be best to resign. Kev has always been one for moving forward and taking chances, and suddenly this seemed like a perfect opportunity. "The change should do us a world of good, and who knows where it will lead," he said.

For my part, I was primarily concerned about Charlie. He was only three years old, and he had a good relationship with his father, and I didn't want to mess that up.

"I'll have to talk to Simon," I said.

"Oh, he won't mind," Kev said. "It'll be a wonderful experience for the little man. And it's a perfect time for it. Before he starts school and everything."

"But he'll miss his dad."

"They actually have phones in America. And e-mail. And we'll bring a computer with a Web cam, so they can see each other."

"What about money?" I said. "I can't afford this."

"I can," he said. "I have some money and I'll sell my car and the apartment."

"Seems a bit radical, doesn't it?"

"Lisa, come on," he said, laughing. "Where's your sense of adventure?"

Before I could commit, I had to call Simon. He was hesitant at first, but I took a cue from Kev and said it would be a marvelous experience for Charlie. "He won't remember a thing," he said. "What do you remember from when you were four years old?" I remembered plenty—the faces in walls of my room, for example— but I didn't mention it. "It's Los Angeles," I said. "There are beaches and Disneyland and the Universal Studios Tour. He'll love it."

Simon slept on it and called me the next day. "I'm going to miss him," he said. "But okay. You can go."

For the next few nights, Kev and I got busy on the Internet, looking for the best possible travel deals, and even managed to find a rental that wasn't far from the beach.

Kev still hadn't decided whether to quit his job or to ask for a three-month leave, and I was worried about my clients, and how they would respond. We were both quite stressed out for the first two weeks, but Kev marched into the house one night and said it was time to put a stop to all this foolishness. "Enough of this. We're going to do it. I'm quitting my job and we're booking the flight tonight and we're going to stop worrying."

We sat down with my appointments diary and worked out when would be a good time to leave. It was only then that I realized I was fully booked until March 2004—I couldn't believe I was booked solid for five months!

Next, we found a flight with Air New Zealand, leaving on March 5 and returning eighty-eight days later, because our U.S. tourist visas would only be valid for ninety days.

"So we're really going to do this?" I asked.

"Too right," Kev said. He fished his wallet out of his pocket and handed me his credit card, and I turned to the computer and finished filling out the requested information. "All we have to do is hit the button that says 'confirm'," I said.

"All right, then. On the count of three."

I shut my eyes, counted to three, and it was done.

We were going to America.

Photo by Kevin Harris

Disneyland

chapter 8

The American Adventure

For the next few months, life proceeded as normal, but everything we did was colored by the coming adventure. "I have a feeling good things are going to happen," Kev said.

"So you're the psychic now, eh?" I said, smiling.

"Maybe it's rubbing off on me. I don't know. But I do feel this is going to be big."

About six weeks before we were to leave, I had to stop taking bookings and Kev began to cancel the ones that coincided with our trip. Most of my clients understood, but some were terribly unhappy about it. They felt as if they were being deserted. "How am I going to make decisions without you?" one of them moaned.

"You've been making your own decisions all along," I said.

"Yes, but based on what you tell me," she retorted.

I saw their point. For many people, readings are a form of psychotherapy. Then again, people survive without their therapists. My job was not to live my clients' lives for them, but to provide information that might point them in the right direction. It's much the same with therapists, I imagine, though of course that advice is rooted in, and limited to, the real world.

"I'm not abandoning you," I said. "And if things get desperate, there's always the telephone."

Kev couldn't stop talking about the trip. He was as excited as a little kid. He suggested I start a journal, and he bought a new, digital camera. He also insisted on getting matching luggage, which I found highly amusing. "We *must* have matching luggage," he said. "It's the only way to go."

Charlie was equally excited. He couldn't stop talking about our promised trips to the beach, and he was over the moon about Disneyland. He said he wanted to go on every single ride, *twice* if there was time for it.

I was strangely calm, though, and Kev couldn't understand why I wasn't getting all giddy with excitement. "I'm telling you," he said, "this trip is going to change our lives."

About a week before the trip, I went to have my hair done, and while I waited my turn, I was writing in my journal. Suddenly I *knew* this trip was going to be huge in so many ways. We really were going away, and there was a good chance this would turn into the adventure of a lifetime! The hairdresser was a girl I hardly knew, but suddenly I found myself telling her about the coming trip. "We're going for three whole months!" I said. "It's going to change our lives!"

When I got home, I went into overdrive: Check and recheck the airplane tickets. Send e-mail confirming the accommodations. Print Google maps. Make tidy piles of California-appropriate clothes. Then I raced around town making purchases for the trip: Reading material for the plane, toiletries, beach toys for Charlie, plane toys, emergency snacks, tourist guides, journal, etc. It wasn't until that night, when I fell into bed exhausted, that my nan's words came back to me: "You'll first make a name for yourself overseas, in America." It was the very same thing the psychic in Kensington

Market had told me! I ran and fetched the spanking new journal and at the top of the first page I wrote: *The American Adventure!*

I thought, *Maybe Kev's right. Maybe Nan and the Kensington Market psychic were right too. Maybe this trip really is going to change our lives!*

When Kev came home that night, he found me in a state of high excitement. "What are you so happy about?" he said.

"It just hit me," I said, jumping up and down.

"What?"

"That we're going to America."

We threw our arms around each other and hugged and danced and laughed. We're going to America! We're *really* going to America!

On the Friday before we left, I did my last two readings, and when my last client left, I just stood there, not knowing what to do with myself! I was relieved but sad, as if I was closing a chapter of my life. I felt like we were already gone. I felt as if I didn't belong in my own house or in my own body. I couldn't wait to leave.

The day before we left, I had an e-mail from the people who had offered us the rental, and they apologized—their plans had fallen through. I was unfazed. I told Kev we'd find a place when we got there, and that it might turn out for the best. We'd at least be able to *see* what we were getting into.

That same night, we had a small gathering at the house, and friends and family came by to wish us well. Charlie got *more* toys, to keep him amused on the plane, and we made arrangement to have Janey stop at the house once a week to keep an eye on things. We gave Mom a key too, and Charlie gave her explicit directions on the care and feeding of his fish. A lot of our friends urged us to get a big, roomy apartment, because they intended to come visit in the very near future.

The following morning, at six, my parents came to the house to drive us to Heathrow Airport, which was about an hour and a half away. We climbed into the car, with our matching luggage, and off we went.

When we got to the airport, Charlie could sense that my mother was a little sad, and he patted her arm and did his best to comfort her. "Nanny, we'll see you soon," he said repeatedly. We checked in and had a bite to eat, and as my parents walked us over to security my mother began to cry. "Mom, it's only three months," I said, fighting my own tears. "We'll be back before you know it."

My father took her arm, we said our good-byes and then walked toward the security check. Just before I went through the metal-detector, however, I turned back to look at them. It was like a scene from a movie: My parents standing there, arm in arm, looking absolutely crushed.

When we got to the gate, Kev took Charlie to the window and showed him the Jumbo Jet that was going to fly us overseas. "Is that going all the way to America?" he asked.

"Yes it is, mate."

"How long does it take?"

"Ten and a half hours," Kev said.

"That's *long*," Charlie said.

I looked over at Kev and smiled. We were a family and it felt right.

The flight over was long but uneventful. The three of us slept, watched movies, ate, and slept some more, and when we arrived at LAX our matching luggage was nowhere to be found. Kev was not happy. It took us two hours to register a claim, but just as we were finishing the paperwork the bags suddenly materialized. We grabbed them, went outside, and were immediately hit by the largeness of everything: the billboards, the cars, the yellow cabs, and of course, the heat. Charlie turned to us and said, "They speak funny over here!" and we started to laugh.

We took a shuttle to an airport hotel and checked in, and the next morning we were jet-lagged and up at 4:00 a.m. We had breakfast, rented a car, got Charlie strapped in—with a mountain of toys—and set off to look for better lodgings.

It was a bit of a shock, to be honest—driving along the freeway. Back in Birmingham, everything was lush and green, and as we pottered along the motorway in our little cars, one would see rolling, sheep-dotted hills in every direction. But in America, it felt as if the billboards had been designed to block out the sky, and everyone drove fantastically huge vehicles with furious intensity. When we finally got off the freeway, however, everything changed, and we realized that California really was just the way it was portrayed in the movies. Well, sort of.

I had been up since four that morning, getting leads on potential apartments though the Internet. Since we didn't know the area, however, we never knew what to expect, and the first place we went to see was more than a little scary. "Crikey," Kev said, as we pulled up in our rental. "I don't think we'll be getting out of the car."

We decided to head toward Santa Monica, because we'd heard so many wonderful things about it, and we kept getting lost. In England, the roads are very clearly marked, and you know well in advance that your exit is coming up. In California, we usually spotted our exit only after we'd driven past it.

Over the course of the next two days, we must have looked at two dozen places—from the sublime to the ridiculous—and finally found a perfect flat on Wilshire and Barrington in West Los Angeles. It had two bedrooms and two bathrooms, and a living room large enough to accommodate the guests we were expecting. The apartment complex also had a gym, tennis courts, and a lovely swimming pool that we knew Charlie would love. We couldn't wait to move in, and the first night, without any furniture, we slept on the floor. The next day we went out and leased everything we needed. The adventure had begun!

For the next three weeks, we did the tourist thing, and all three of us fell in love with America. We went to Disneyland, to the various beaches (not that I swam, mind you—I'm deathly afraid of the ocean even though I can swim like a fish), for hikes in the mountains, for leisurely strolls along Rodeo Drive, and we lounged by the pool, watching Charlie pretend to be a dolphin. We also met many locals and Kev and I agreed that we loved their natural enthusiasm and friendliness.

I did some readings, too, for people who we met around the pool and in the local restaurant. I also had calls from several clients back home, who were struggling with separation anxiety, and I did my best to calm them down.

On the second week, our friends Chris and Linzi came over, as threatened, and we showed them around the city and planned a trip to Vegas. One night we left Charlie with the sitter, whom he adored, and the four of us went out to dinner. I had a little too much to drink and I remember feeling happy as I looked across the table at my man, who was deep in conversation. "Kev," I said, calling out to him over the din, and perhaps slurring a little. "When we go to Vegas shall we get married?"

He laughed. "Don't be so silly, Lisa!" he said, and carried on with his conversation.

I was devastated, but he didn't even notice, and Linzi took me to the ladies' room and did her best to comfort me. "Don't let it bother you," she said. "The guy doesn't know a good thing when he's on to one."

And nothing more was said on the subject.

The following week we all took off for Vegas—to gamble a bit, not to get married—but by then I'd resigned myself to single motherhood, and I didn't give the matter another thought. Well, not *much*, anyway. As for Kev, he remained genuinely oblivious. We were standing in front of the roulette wheel at one point, and he said, "I'm putting a hundred on black."

"It's going to be red," I said.

"Don't do that!" he said. "I've already made up my mind."

He bet on black and it came up red.

"You should listen to me," I said, and went off to play blackjack.

I did very well. I knew when I was going to bust, and I always knew when the dealer had twenty-one, so I didn't lose a single hand. I was loving it, but Kev and our friends had finished their gambling and were eager to get going. Needless to say, I was the only one who came out of Vegas winning!

The week after our friends left, we found a wonderful local pre-school for Charlie, and the day he started we had more visitors from home—our good friend Anita, and her brother, Gopi. Anita was about to turn thirty, and she had timed the trip so that we could celebrate together.

It was the Thursday before her birthday and I woke up feeling unwell. Kev took Anita and Gopi shopping and I stayed in bed most of the day, hoping to be back in fighting form in time for Anita's birthday bash. By midday, I was feeling worse, and my lower stomach had begun to ache, so I tried to do a little Reiki on myself. I went though my series of symbols, as dictated by the practice, and tried, literally, to *lift* the pain out of me. It worked for a short while, but wouldn't completely go away.

Kev, meanwhile, had taken a break from shopping to go and see a local dentist about a cracked tooth. By the time he got back to the apartment, the Novocain was beginning to wear off and his tooth hurt like hell again. Then I remembered how I'd helped Anne's Mom, Sally, with her toothache, so I reached up and put my hand against Kev's jaw. A moment later, his eyes went wide. "What did you just do?" he said. "The pain's completely gone!"

"I don't know," I said. "I tried the same thing on my stomach, and it didn't do much good."

Later that night, Kev and I joined Anita and Gopi for dinner. I still felt lousy, but I didn't want to let them down. But in mid-meal the pain was so intense that Kev had to take me back to the apartment. We sent the babysitter home, and I lay down, but the pain only got worse. I eventually drifted off and had a very vivid dream in which I saw myself dancing in a wedding dress. It seemed like a very happy dream, except that suddenly someone, or something—I couldn't see who or what—was stabbing me repeatedly in the back. I woke up in an agony of pain. It was five o'clock in the morning and Kev was already awake. I had woken him with my moaning. Charlie was asleep on a mattress at the foot of the bed, since Anita and Gopi had taken his room.

"This is killing me," I said. "I'm going to take a hot shower to see if that helps."

I took the shower, but it didn't help, and when I returned Kev went to touch my stomach. The pain was so intense I cursed and pulled away. "Jesus," I said. "I can't take it anymore. This is excruciating."

Charlie woke up at 6:30 and came over to my side. "Are you okay, Mommy?" he asked.

"I'm fine," I said.

"No, you're not," he said. "You need to go to the hospital."

"He's right," Kev said. "We need to find you a doctor."

Kev got Charlie ready for school, and the three of us went downstairs to get into the car, with me bent over like a ninety-year-old lady. When we dropped Charlie off, Kev went in and asked for the nearest hospital, and he was told to take me to the UCLA Medical Center, in Westwood, less than ten minutes away. They said to go directly to the emergency room, which is what we did.

By the time we got there, I was in such pain I could hardly walk. After filling out the necessary paperwork, a nurse took my pulse, which was 120, and my blood pressure was dangerously high.

I was quickly wheeled into an examining room, where a young doctor came in and gave me morphine for the pain. I drifted off, and when I woke up about thirty minutes later, Kev was still by my side, holding my hand.

Another doctor came in, and as he examined me, for some reason I noticed the picture on the far wall. It showed a dying flower, surrounded by fallen petals. I'm sure it was nice enough, but I thought it was inappropriate for a hospital.

"On a scale of one to ten," the doctor said, "how bad is the pain?"

The nurse had asked me the same question an hour earlier and I told her it was at eleven, but now the pain was getting worse. "A twelve," I said, crying.

He gave me another shot of morphine, and said he'd be back in a few minutes, but it didn't help. I was in agony. Just as the pain was becoming unbearable, I looked up and saw my grandmother floating above the foot of the bed. There was a powerful, bright light behind her, as white a white as I'd ever seen, and I was immediately drawn to it. I felt myself lift off the bed and float toward my grandmother, literally feeling myself pulled toward the light. As I floated, the pain went further and further away. It was such a wonderful relief. I felt peaceful and content, and my nan was smiling at me with such tenderness that I felt like I was being welcomed into the comfort of home.

My grandmother held my hands and said, "Go back."

I understood what she was saying, but I didn't want to go back. I was feeling so much better, I didn't want to go back to the pain.

"Go back," she repeated. "It's not your time yet. You have too much work ahead of you."

She wanted me to stay away from the light, and to return to the hospital bed, but I was tired of hurting. "I can't," I said. "The pain is too bad."

"I know," she said. "But you're going to be okay. I promise."

She came closer and hugged me. I wanted to stay there forever, but a moment later I felt the sharp intensity of the pain return. I looked around and couldn't understand why I was alone in the room. Then I heard Kev's voice booming from the corridor: "Someone get a doctor in here now!" It reminded me of the last time I'd been in this much pain, back home, when my father took me to the hospital on Boxing Day.

Kev came back in, trying to act calm. He stroked my arm and my head and told me it was going to be all right—that someone was coming. By this time, I was sobbing. I could feel hot tears running down the sides of my face.

I thought of Charlie and what his life would be like without me. "I don't want to die," I said finally, and Kev had to lean in close to hear me. He replied, "Don't worry, darling, you're going to be okay. I'll make sure of that."

A nurse came in with another shot of morphine, and the next thing I knew I was waking up in a different room. Kev was by my side. I was hooked up to a morphine drip, and he explained that I could push a little button for relief whenever I felt pain. I pushed the button right away, and I don't believe I stopped pushing it for several hours.

Before long, Kev left to go get Charlie, assuring me that he'd be back first thing in the morning. He kissed me on the forehead and walked out, and I felt very alone. I hated watching him go, but Charlie needed him, and at that point there wasn't much he could do for me.

I woke up at four in the morning, which would have made it noon in Birmingham. I called my mother and told her I was in the hospital, but she already knew—Kev had called her. She had been waiting to hear from me so she could hop on the next plane to Los Angeles. "No," I said. "I'm going to be okay." But on the inside I was crying, crying like a little girl and thinking, *I want my mom. My mom is going to make it all better. No one can take care of you like your mom.*

Still, talking to her made me feel a little better, and by the end of the day I was not in as much pain. The doctors had found a horrid infection in my fallopian tubes, and it took four full days of intravenous antibiotics before they started working.

Kev and Charlie came to visit every day, and Kev would bring me food from outside—a nice big Jamba Juice, or an English cheese-and-pickle sandwich. Charlie would sit next to the bed and draw pictures or watch TV with me.

On the fifth day, I begged the doctor to let me go. "If you can walk to the end of the corridor on your own, you can go home," she said.

Two days later, determined to go home, I hobbled outside and made the long, endless walk, and they discharged me that same afternoon. They gave me loads of antibiotics and loads of Vicodin and made me promise to return at the first hint of pain. I remember how relieved I was when Kev and Charlie wheeled me out of the hospital, Charlie on one side, Kev on the other, both of them as eager as I was to get me out of there.

That night, when Kev and I got into bed, he turned to me and said, "Do you remember what you told me back home, during that reading?"

"Which part?" I said.

"You predicted that I'd be going overseas, and that there would be other people with me, and that one of them would have a near-death experience," he said.

"You're right," I said. "I'd forgotten."

"You scare me sometimes," he said.

"Sometimes I scare myself!" I said.

When I felt better, if not wholly recovered, we visited San Diego, followed by a week in Vancouver, and fell in love with both places. When we got home, I stopped in at the hospital for a follow-up visit. The pain was less intense, but it hadn't gone entirely, and sometimes it came on me unawares, as if I were being stabbed. The doctors were stymied. The infection was much improved, but it hadn't gone away entirely.

That same week, my celebrity client invited us to the House of Blues, on Sunset Boulevard, to watch him perform. After the show, we met him in the Green Room, where he was surrounded by friends and some fans. He introduced us to his friends, saying, "Do you remember me telling you about Lisa? The clairvoyant?"

Next thing I knew, Kev and I were sitting with a small group of his friends and they were all asking me questions about my work. *What is it like in the spirit world? Are my loved ones around me all the time? Can you switch off and have a life away from it?*

In the space of a week, I did eight readings for his friends, including a reading for the stepdaughter of a famous, long-dead actress. I had no idea who she was, nor the mother who came through in spirit, and it wasn't until Kev came back and started talking to her that we realized who they were.

I did a reading for a well-known DJ, telling her she'd be packing her bags and moving to Europe. She wanted to believe me and I made it sound so easy, but she wasn't sure whether I was just telling her something she wanted to hear. As it turned out, I was correct because within six months she was living in Spain.

And I did a reading for a woman who had lost her father and brother in an accident, and who had never had a chance to say good-bye. Both of them appeared to us that night, and when she left she was weeping with gratitude.

Before long, I was hearing from complete strangers, people who knew people who knew someone who'd met me at the House of Blues, and I was booking two readings a day. That was my limit, though. I was on vacation with Kev and Charlie, and I didn't want to overdo it.

Then suddenly the pain returned, and I found myself back at UCLA Medical Center, conferring with my female gynecologist. As she examined me, we made small talk, and I told her I was a medium. She didn't bat an eye, so clearly she was open to it. "Let me ask you something," she said. "Did you do any healing on yourself before you came to the hospital that first night?"

"Yes," I said. "Well, I tried, anyway. It didn't help."

"You're wrong," she said. "Given the severity of your infection, it's hard to believe your fallopian tube didn't rupture. You're lucky to be alive."

"But now I'm cleared up, right?"

"No," she said. "We need to operate."

I was shocked at the news. "I don't have the time," I said. "We're flying back to London the week after next, on May 28."

"I'm not going to let you spend ten hours on a plane in this condition. It's too risky, you could die on the flight."

That really scared me. I couldn't believe our stay was turning into such a nightmare.

She scheduled an operation for May 26 and told me I'd need at least ten days to recover. We would have to apply to the US Embassy to extend our visas, which, we were told, would be no easy feat. However, when something is meant to be, things seem to fall into place. We went to the embassy expecting a full day of red tape and questioning. But when I explained my situation to the gentleman behind the desk, he simply took our passports and the cover letter from the hospital, and two minutes later returned from a back office, our visas stamped for an extra ten days. Call it fate, luck, or divine intervention; whatever it was, we couldn't believe it!

The day before the operation, a lady reached me on my mobile. "My name is Lauren," she said. "You met my daughter at the House of Blues, and subsequently read for her. She was very impressed and recommended I come see you. Can you see me tomorrow?"

"Unfortunately, I'm having surgery tomorrow," I said, laughing. "I'll need the weekend to recover, but maybe you could come Tuesday. How does three o'clock sound?"

"Perfect," she said.

On the morning of the operation, we ran into a problem with the insurance company in the UK. They told the hospital that I should be stabilized and put on a plane home, despite the fact that it could kill me. They also insisted on obtaining second opinions from various different doctors, all of whom were miles away. I was distressed, and even the usually calm Kev was pacing up and down. My doctor suggested we talk to her boss, Dr. Berwick, to see if he could help us with the insurance situation.

Dr. Berwick, the most eminent doctor in his field, kindly read my notes, took one look at me, and said, "There is no question you need this operation. Go through to the emergency room now, and I'll make sure everything is set up for you." I couldn't believe my ears. Immensely relieved, I cried and gave him a big hug. and Kev shook his hand and offered his heartfelt thanks.

The operation was a complete success. Through a laparoscopy my fallopian tubes were reopened, and the infection was cleared away. Once I recovered from the procedure, I was sent on my way. I felt the staff at UCLA had saved my life, and I went around thanking everyone for all they'd done for me.

Photo by Barbara Icaza

I spent enough time there—we bought T-shirts!

I spent the next few days recuperating, part of it in Malibu, on the beach, where I watched from a safe distance as Kev and Charlie frolicked in the water.

Tuesday at three, as scheduled, Lauren arrived at our apartment for her reading. Charlie was at school, and Kev went off to the pool to give us some privacy.

The reading went well, and when it was over Lauren told me she was very impressed. "I know someone who will be interested in meeting you. Have you ever done any TV work?" she asked.

"No," I said quizzically.

"Well, this gentleman is in the television business, and I work for him. He is developing a project that would be perfect for you."

"I'd be delighted to meet him," I said. "Just let me know when." I must admit I was feeling very skeptical about this—after all, this is Hollywood: small fish, big pond, bigger ideas.

She left my apartment at 5:00 and I honestly didn't expect to hear from her again, but she rang within twenty minutes. "It's Lauren," she said. "I've had a word with him, and he wants to meet you tomorrow at two. Are you available?"

"Absolutely," I said, trying to sound as convincing at I could.

She gave me directions—she told me to valet park at the Regent Beverly Wilshire, at the foot of Rodeo Drive, and to make my way across the street to their offices.

"You'll be meeting with Merv Griffin," she said. "You know who he is, of course."

"No," I said. "I'm sorry. I don't."

She laughed. "You may want to Google him before you come over."

"Thanks, I will," I said, and we said our good-byes. As I hung up, Kev was coming though the door. "Have you ever heard of Merv Griffin?" I asked him.

"Merv Griffin? Yes, I think so. I think he's in the entertainment business. Maybe an actor."

I was about to Google him, but I saw the time. We were meeting friends for drinks and an early dinner, so I went off to shower and dress. We met at a club at Hollywood and Vine, then had dinner, and as the evening began to wind down my friend asked me if I'd have lunch with her the following day. "I can't," I said. "I have a meeting with Merv Griffin." She nearly choked on her drink!

"You have a meeting with who?" one of the girls asked.

"Merv Griffin," I repeated. "Do you know him?"

"He's only one of the biggest television producers around!"

When Kev and I got home, we Googled Merv and were absolutely gobsmacked. He was a singer, actor, writer, composer, and producer, with a list of credits that went on forever. I'd never seen any of his work back in England, but I'd heard of *Wheel of Fortune* and *Jeopardy!*, and those two shows were just the tip of the iceberg.

"Bloody hell," Kev said. "This guy is a legend!"

"I know!" I said.

"You must have really impressed that Lauren woman."

"I don't see how," I said. "It was just a normal reading to me."

"Well, maybe his will be better."

"But I'm not sure it's a reading he wants," I said. "Lauren asked me if I'd ever done TV."

"That's weird."

"You know what's even weirder? My nan told me about him. She said there would be two older men in my life. One I'd marry, the other would open doors."

"Well, thank God I'm not older," Kev joked. "So you're either going to marry this guy, or he's going to open some doors for you."

The following afternoon, Kev drove me to Beverly Hills, parked at the Regent Beverly Wilshire, and walked me across the street to Merv's office. That's as far as he went. He gave me a kiss and wished me good luck, and I told him I'd call the minute it was over.

I walked into the big, yellow building and told the receptionist that my name was Lisa Williams, and that I was there to see Mr. Griffin. "Yes," she said. "He's expecting you." She buzzed someone, and a moment later a young man appeared and ushered me into an elevator. We went up one floor. I remember thinking, *One floor! We should have walked!*

When the elevator opened, Merv's assistant, Michael, introduced himself and we stood talking briefly in the corridor. While I was chatting, I noticed that the walls to either side of us were crowded with photographs—Merv with famous celebrities—and that the surrounding shelves were filled with awards. I later discovered that most of these were Emmys, and there were more than a dozen of them.

"Merv will see you now," he said, and he turned and led me toward the office.

A moment later, I was ushered past a set of wooden doors into a huge, loftlike room. To my left, I saw a sofa that ran from one wall to the next, and to my right I saw a huge oak desk, the biggest desk I'd ever seen in my life. Merv Griffin was seated behind it. When he saw me, his eyes lit up, and he got to his feet. He was a big, solid guy with a shock of white hair, and there was a large, fluffy dog at his side. He approached and gave me a big hug. "Lisa, it is very nice to meet you," he said in a lovely, warm voice.

"It's nice to meet you, too," I said.

There were four chairs lined up in front of Merv's massive desk, and he indicated the one he wanted me to take. Lauren was there, with a colleague, and we exchanged quick hellos. We all took our seats, and when I looked up I found Merv studying me with great intensity. For a moment, I forgot that there were other people in the room. "Lisa, I've heard so many wonderful things about you," he said, pausing to gesture toward Lauren. "I want to thank you for coming."

"Thank you for having me," I said. "And I want to apologize. I honestly didn't know very much about you until last night, when I Googled you."

He laughed. "That's all right," he said. "My shows never went to the U.K., but there are no hard feelings. I actually own a castle in Ireland." He picked up a copy of *Hello!* magazine, which of course I was familiar with, and flipped it open. There was a big article on Merv, and photographs of him at his spectacular house in La Quinta, which is just south of Palm Springs. "My God," I said. "I would hate to have to clean that house!"

"Lisa," he said. "I have people to clean the house."

Everyone had a good laugh, then Merv turned suddenly serious. "Do you see a spirit of anyone in this room?" he asked.

"Yes," I said. "There's a lady sitting on the sofa there."

"What does she look like?"

I described her, down to the jewelry she was wearing, and Merv was taken aback. "That's my mother, all right." He looked over at Lauren, to signal that he was impressed, then turned back to me. "Tell me a little bit about how you work," he said.

I gave him a brief history—that I'd started out as a psychic, using the gifts I'd inherited from my grandmother, Frances Glazebrook, and that I did a bit of everything. Tarot, psychometry, communicating with the dead, clairvoyance, and so on. "I go where the spirits take me," I said.

"Well, I'm very interested in that whole world, and I have an idea for a TV show," he said. "I hope I might interest you in becoming a part of it."

"I'm already very interested," I said.

"I've been doing a lot of research into the field. Psychics, mediums, astrologers, handwriting analysts—the works. I'm going to put something together, and it's going to include you. You have a wonderful face for television, and I have an eye for talent."

"Thank you," I said.

After giving a reading and some healing to one of his executives, Merv stood, signaling that the meeting was drawing to a close, and walked me to the elevator. "It has been an absolute pleasure meeting you today," he said.

"Likewise," I said.

He pressed the call button and turned to face me, the big dog at his side. "I have just one more question for you, and I need to ask it because it baffles me," he said. "Why aren't you famous yet?"

"Because I've never met you, Merv!"

Merv laughed and gave me a big hug, as the elevator arrived.

"You will be hearing from me very soon," he said.

"I hope so," I said, as the elevator doors closed, shutting him from view.

I was still grinning when I reached the street.

Photo © Andrew Thomas

Wedding day

chapter 9

Wedding Bells

The meeting with Merv Griffin had lasted almost two hours, but for me it had gone by in a flash. Kev, on the other hand, had been waiting for an eternity. "I thought you'd be gone for twenty minutes!" he said when we met on a nearby corner. "What happened?"

"Good things," I said, and told him everything.

We had one week left in California, and we made the best of it. We went to the beaches, did a little shopping, and spent time with our new American friends. The night before we left, a big group of us went out for a good-bye dinner at The Little Door on 3rd Street, and as it was winding down I made a toast and said, "I'll see all of you in September!"

"You're coming back in September?"

"Actually, I don't know why I said that. The words just popped out of me. But if I said it—or if someone *helped* me say it—it must be true."

Then we flew back to England, with our matching luggage, and I got back to work. Before I knew it my waiting list was back up to three months again.

We reconnected with some friends, including Mike, Kev's friend, who we knew had met someone. However, we never expected to be greeted from our trip with an invite to his wedding, which was to take place on my birthday. As I opened the invitation, I laughed and reminded him of what I had said to him a few years earlier. "See, you didn't believe me when I told you I would be at your wedding!"

Once we were settled back home, I booked an appointment with my doctor, who reviewed what had happened to me, and agreed that I was lucky to be alive. I told her what the American doctor had said, about the Reiki, for one thing, but I could see she wasn't a big believer, so I dropped it. She booked a follow-up and sent me on my way.

Unlike my doctor, I was more interested than ever in the healing arts, and was determined to explore them further. In short order I was presented with two opportunities. The first involved a new client who had been diagnosed with chronic fatigue syndrome and was chronically short of breath. When we were done with the reading, I had her lay on the sofa and placed my hands on her midsection, just below her lungs. I was barely touching her, but she said she could feel the energy from my hands pulsing against her, and she began to relax. After a minute of this, she sat up and took a deep breath and said she felt strangely energized. It may well have been the power of suggestion, or even wishful thinking on her part, but she definitely looked like a woman transformed.

The second opportunity concerned a new client who had come to see me to ask if there was a child in her future. I didn't immediately see one, and I told her so. She said it was probably her fault. She said she was frightened by the responsibilities of motherhood, and worried about doing a good job, and that as a result she was blocking the very idea of pregnancy. But she and her husband genuinely wanted a child, and she felt she was ready—on a conscious level, anyway. The other part of her, the subconscious part, remained hesitant and frightened. I said I thought I might be able to help, and I had her lay on the sofa. I ran my hands up and down her body, trying to release the blockage, and at one point I saw tiny dots of light—like small, translucent raindrops—leaving her body through the top of her head. I don't know what they were, but I know I saw them, and three months later she called with wonderful news: She was pregnant.

I had one other very strange experience during this period, unrelated to healing, but interesting nonetheless. It involved an Asian-Indian woman who lived in Birmingham. I had been booked for a group reading, and this woman was the hostess. I did three readings for her guests in quick succession. By the time I got to her, I was feeling very tired, which made me feel a bit guilty, but I proceeded anyway. I asked her if she wanted to know everything, turned on the recorder, and we got started. Not more than a few minutes into it, overcome with exhaustion, I closed my eyes—promising myself that it would only be for a minute. But I dozed off and woke a bit later with a start. "I am so sorry," I said. She was staring at me, open-mouthed. "It has been a very long day, I'm tired, so maybe we should do this another day." The recorder was still running. She didn't respond, she just sat there staring at me. "Are you okay?" I said.

"Do you not know what just happened?" she said.

"I think I went to sleep."

"Listen to the recording," she said.

I did as she told me to, and something had indeed happened. A man's voice could be heard, speaking in Punjabi, but there was no man in the room. It was *me* talking. Now it was my turn to be shocked. I knew a little something about channeling, and I myself had been known to pick up accents and mannerisms during the course of a reading, but I'd never experienced anything like this.

"Do I sound like anyone you know?" I asked.

"Yes," she said. "My late grandfather."

I asked her to translate what he had said, and she did: He was telling her that she needn't worry because the treatment would be successful.

"Does that make any sense to you?" I said. "Because it makes no sense to me."

"Yes," she said. "A few weeks ago I was diagnosed with breast cancer, and I was sure I was going to die." She had tears in her eyes. "That is when I booked my reading."

"It seems you're not going to die after all," I said, smiling.

"I don't know how to thank you," she said, crying openly now.

I reached over and patted her hand. "Don't thank me. I didn't do much. Thank your granddad."

The following week, realizing I hadn't had a reading of my own in a very long time, I decided to go to a group session at the Harborne Healing Center, my grandmother's old hangout. On Saturday nights, it's like a village hall, and different psychics, mediums, and clairvoyants take to the stage over the course of the evening. Kev came with me. I was wearing a red top I'd bought in America, hoping that someone would pick up some signals and let me know I was on the right track with all that TV business. I hadn't heard anything from Merv, and I knew these things took time, but I wanted to see if America was really in the cards. It was all about clarification, really.

The woman who took the stage said there was someone in the room who knew someone who had a cross tattooed on his earlobe. I had a cousin with a tattoo on his earlobe, but I wasn't sure it was a cross, and I hadn't seen him in ages, so I was fairly sure it wasn't me. But then she pointed at me and said, "It's you there. In back. The lady with the red top."

"Me?" I said, pointing at myself, a little surprised.

She nodded and went on: "I also have a gentleman here, whose name is Jack, and he's telling me he's your grandfather." Now it was getting interesting, but there was more. "And I have a lady here, strong, dominant, who seems very much at home in this environment." That was good, if a bit vague. "She's telling me that you need to be patient. It's going to work out, so give it time."

At this point I was still relatively unimpressed. Anyone can tell you to give it time, to be patient, because all of us are always waiting for something to happen, even if it's not monumental—even if it's something as fleeting as a dinner party. But then she dropped the bomb: "Her name is Frances. Does that name mean anything to you?"

Everyone turned to have a look at me. They all knew Frances, who'd been a bit of a legend in her day, and now they knew who I was. Of course, I can imagine what you're thinking. I was a local medium; people knew me; someone had recognized me and said something to the lady before she went on stage. And I myself was thinking that very thing. But then the lady on stage really clinched it. "Frances says she's glad to see you're finally doing the work you're meant to be doing," she said. "And the answer to your question is, *Yes*. You *will* be going to America."

There was no way any of them knew about *that*.

In mid-July, Charlie's dad got married, and Charlie went off to attend the wedding. I was glad Simon had included him. Kev and I, meanwhile, settled in for a quiet, domestic weekend. On Friday, we went for a curry at the Dhakra, a local Indian restaurant, and the owner, Abdul, lit up when he saw us. "The usual, guys?" he said, beaming.

"The usual," we replied with anticipation.

After dinner, well sated, we drove home and went to bed, and the following day we lounged around the house, reading, watching TV, and picking at leftover chicken masala. At around seven that night, some friends rang, and we went off to join them for drinks and a bit of dancing. Kev and I found ourselves alone at the bar at one point, taking a breather, and suddenly he turned to me and said, "Lisa, when we go back to America, shall we get married?"

I looked at him, puzzled. "Are you proposing to me?"

He smiled. "I suppose so," he said.

"How romantic!" I said. I was being a tad sarcastic, admittedly, but I was actually very happy. I got off my stool and hugged and kissed him, but my elation was tempered by a single, horrifying thought: *How many drinks has Kev had, and is this the drink talking?*

"You're not going to back out in the morning, are you?" I asked.

"No! Of course not! Let's do this. Let's get married."

I hugged and kissed him again, with considerably more enthusiasm this time, but then another thought entered my mind: *Oh my God! He's serious! How terrifying!*

Poor bugger couldn't win.

At this point we saw our friends returning from the dance floor, and Kev said, "Let's tell them."

So we did. "Kev has just proposed to me," I said. "We're getting married."

There were hugs and kisses all around, and a few squeals of delight thrown in for good measure.

"Did he get down on one knee?" one friend asked.

"No," I said.

"I thought about it and it's the thought that counts," Kev said jokingly.

"You know what this means, don't you?" my girlfriend said, beaming. "It means you're going shopping for an engagement ring."

"No," Kev said. "There will be no engagement ring. I don't believe in engagement rings. We're going straight to marriage."

The next day we shared the news with my family, and everyone was delighted.

We weren't sure when we wanted to get married, but neither of us wanted to wait too long.

The very next day, I went online and started hunting around for a suitable venue, and I noticed that they held weddings at the Birmingham Botanical Gardens. I thought that would be a lovely idea, since we wanted to keep it small and intimate, but Kev wasn't convinced. "All right," I said. "We'll argue about it later."

But we didn't argue. We seldom argued. We were both very happy. I went around telling everyone that I was engaged, and they were thrilled for me, but the hugs and kisses were invariably followed by the same question: "Where's your engagement ring, then?" I didn't have one, of course, and I tried to explain: "Kev doesn't believe in engagement rings." People would nod sagely, and say "I see," but others assumed Kev was just being cheap. They were wrong. I can tell you that he is anything but cheap—he is the most generous man I've ever met—and the accusations began to wear thin. In very short order, I found myself agreeing with Kev. Why did I need an engagement ring? I *knew* I was engaged. I didn't need a ring to remind me.

Charlie was absolutely over the moon when we told him. It meant Kevin would be there *all the time,* and he'd never have to wish him good-night over the phone.

That same week, the three of us went off to the Botanical Gardens, to take a look at the venue, and all three of us thought it was perfect. Our favorite room was one of the smaller ones, which could accommodate up to sixty guests, and it was actually available on Saturday, October 30.

"Next year, right?" Kev said, thinking he had at least a year to prepare.

"No," we were told. "*This* year."

Kev went a little pale, as you can imagine, but he recovered, and we booked the room straightaway. But after we booked it, the coordinator told us we'd need a magistrate to marry us, and that she didn't hold out much hope of finding one on such short notice. Once again, fate stepped in. We phoned the magistrate's office, and discovered, unbelievably, they'd just had a cancellation and a registrar was available at noon, October 30—precisely the time we needed her. "Oh my God," Kevin said. "There are no coincidences in life, are there!"

I then went off to look for a proper wedding dress, and my friend Anita suggested we have a look around Soho Road, which is very Asian. We went into one store, and when I looked around I realized I was the only English person there. I remember thinking, *If I slip into a trance right now, I'll be able to speak fluent Punjabi!*

I ended up finding a snug, ivory-colored sari, beautifully embroidered, that went all the way down to my ankles. I was told that they had to take a few measurements which they would be faxing over to India, and that I could come back for it in six weeks. I plunked down four hundred pounds and left in a bit of a daze, wondering what I'd just done. "I'm going to need someone to come and wrap me up on the big day," I told Anita.

When I got home, I didn't tell Kev about the sari, and he knew better than to ask. We got busy arranging the flowers, the music, and the food. "We're having bangers and mash and cheesecake, our favorites," I said. For the uninitiated, bangers are sausages, mash is potatoes, and cheesecake is cheesecake the world over. We even designed our own invitations.

In the midst of this, I got an e-mail from Lauren, the producer who'd introduced me to Merv, asking if I'd be willing to fly back to the States in September. They were going to shoot a television pilot for the show Merv had discussed with me, and they were calling it *The Predictors*.

"September?" Kev said. "Isn't that what you told everyone on our last night in Los Angeles? 'I'll see you in September.'"

I flew to LA three weeks later, and got ready for the pilot. I was told I would be sharing the stage with another psychic/medium, an astrologer, a handwriting analyst, and a numerologist, and that we would be doing random readings for members of the audience. That Friday, the five of us filed onto the stage, looking like game-show panelists, and took our seats. Everyone in the audience had been asked to supply their birth dates and full names for the numerologist, and to write a complete sentence—using all the letters in the alphabet—for the handwriting analyst. The producers of the show picked eight people at random, and we were asked, as a group, to choose the person we most wanted to speak to. I wanted to speak to a man called Dennis, but I was outvoted by the others, who selected a man called Walter. My fellow panelists proceeded to tell Walter all sorts of things about his life, which very much impressed the audience, and then we took a break.

We also had a celebrity guest who was invited along to get a "reading" and I was the first one up, feeling very nervous. I proceeded to tell him some things which he made jokes about, until I mentioned his mother's father, who had not long passed. He was telling the guest that he was going to go far and be very successful. Suddenly the guest stopped cracking the jokes and started to listen very intently, quite shocked at what I was saying.

During the intermission, I ran around looking for Dennis, and I found him, but he seemed more interested in the astrologer and the numerologist. I addressed him anyway, and I made it quick: "I just want to tell you that someone you know, someone you're close to, has been fighting cancer recently, and that I've been told that everything is going to be okay," I said.

There were people within earshot, and they were whispering among themselves—*Cancer? What did she tell him? Is someone unwell?*—but I was focused solely on Dennis. For several moments he just stared at me, saying nothing, then he took me aside, so we could talk in private. "Ms. Williams," he whispered, "I don't know how you did that, but I just had a tumor removed last week, and it was malignant."

"Well, you have nothing to worry about," I said, smiling.

When the show resumed, members of the audience were urged to ask us questions, and the first one was put to me. "Lisa," a lady said. "Can you communicate with my mother?"

"I have a lady here," I said. "Her name is Betty."

The woman gasped and started crying. "That's her! That's my mother!"

I felt badly for her, so I left my seat and went into the audience, and the various cameramen followed me, scrambling to get this on film. I took the woman's hand. "Your mother is telling me that she's fine, but she misses sitting in your kitchen eating cookies," I said. The woman could only sob, overwrought, and I gave her a big hug and returned to my seat, with the cameras still following me.

I had no sooner rejoined the panel when a second woman stood and addressed me. "Lisa, I'd like to communicate with my nephew."

"Your nephew was murdered, wasn't he?"

She nodded, numb, and a cry went up from the crowd.

There was a third question, also for me, and I became a bit embarrassed. There were four other people on the panel, all with talents of their own, and I didn't want this to turn into *The Lisa Williams Show*.

After another brief intermission, Merv asked each of us to make a prediction for the year to come. I can't remember what the other panelists predicted, but I clearly remember what I said: "There's going to be a huge natural disaster in the Far East, toward the end of the year. Thailand, China—somewhere over there. Many people will lose their lives, but it's going to bring the nations together to help." As usual, I was unclear on what that meant, and I was unable to explain it further. Merv said, "That's not a very cheerful prediction, is it?" And I replied, "No, but it's what came to me."

As the show wrapped up, and we made our way back to the dressing rooms, Merv's assistant intercepted me and said his boss wanted to talk to me. I thought I was in trouble. I thought he was going to reprimand me for breaking the rules by leaving the stage and making direct contact with the audience, and by inadvertently monopolizing the second part of the show, so I braced myself for the worst. When I walked into the dressing room, I found him surrounded by friends, family, and assorted well-wishers, and I hoped I wasn't going to receive a public scolding. He lit up when he saw me, and reached out and took my hand. "Ah, Lisa!" he said.

"H-have I done something wrong?" I stammered.

"No, no," he said. "Not at all. I just wanted to get you away from everyone. I know they are dying to bombard you with questions, and I was just trying to protect you."

I felt greatly relieved. "That's very kind," I said.

Then Lauren appeared at our side. "You know, Lisa, given what we saw, we can see you having your own show. You're a natural."

"Really?" I said, somewhat shocked.

"Really," Merv said.

I went back to the hotel and called Kev at home and told him everything, including my prediction about the disaster. "You need to document that in an e-mail," he said.

"Why?" I said. "The show was taped."

"Please, just do it," he said. "You never know."

I rang off and did indeed send the e-mail Kev had suggested after I returned from LA. The e-mail was dated September 14, 2004.

The following morning, I packed my bags and flew home to England, to get on with my life, and a week later I heard from Lauren: Merv had hated the show, she said, and it would never air. "But don't despair," she added. "He is still very interested in you."

I went about my life, trying not to think about Merv, or about America, but it was clearly on my mind: One day I heard that a well-known psychic was coming to town, to do an evening demonstration, and I rang my mom and told her I was going to get us a pair of tickets.

On the night in question, we turned up at this little social club in Redditch that was hosting the event. The moment I walked in, I was recognized by several of my clients, and it felt a little odd to have people nodding in my direction and muttering God knows what. "Let's sit near the back," I told my mom, and we found seats in the second-to-last row. I was trying to be inconspicuous, but I felt bad for Mom: She had lost a brother a year earlier, and she had lost her mother, and on the drive over she had said she hoped she might receive a message from at least one of them. Right off, however, I could see that this psychic was a bit of a showman, and it put me off. He was walking around the room with a wireless mike, pattering on and making little jokes, but every once in a while he'd get a name right and start fishing around for information. "I see you were very close. . . . Exchanged presents at Christmas . . . Went out to dinner on festive occasions . . ."

At one point, I excused myself and went to the loo, and as I was washing my hands I saw the vague shape of a man in the corner. "You need to tell your mom I'm here," the man said.

"Who are you?" I said.

"Just tell her it's Jim. She'll know."

I hurried back to my seat and leaned close to my mom and whispered, "Mom, there's a guy in the loo who wants to talk to you. Says his name is Jim."

"Jim?" she says. "Jim?" And then it hits her. "Oh my God, that's your aunt's brother. He passed away quite young."

Suddenly Nan appeared. She smiled at me, saying nothing, then turned her attention to Mom. "Do you have the ring?" she asked.

I looked at my mom, but I realized she couldn't hear her. "Nan's here," I said. "She wants to know if you have the ring."

"I can't believe you just said that," Mom said, startled. "How do you know about the ring?"

"I don't know about it. It's Nan that's asking."

I looked up and Nan was gone, and, behind us, I could still the psychic-comedian prancing about the room, trying to get laughs and fishing for information. I turned back to my mom and said, "If that guy was really any good, he would have seen Nan."

"You're right," she said. "He's not much cop."

We stayed for the whole show anyway, disappointing as it was, and when it was over made our way into the parking lot. Just as we reached the car, Mom stopped me, opened her purse, and handed me a ring. It was her grandmother's ring, passed down to her by Nan, and it was quite lovely: A simple gold band with six small diamonds embedded along the top. "I know it's been getting you down—people asking you about an engagement ring," she said. "I want you to have this."

I was very moved, and I couldn't stop thanking her, and the following day I went off to have it sized. Kev still didn't believe in engagement rings, but he understood the sentiment, and I wore it proudly.

On Wednesday, October 27, three days before the wedding, I had a really horrible morning. I'd been down to pick up my sari, which was absolutely stunning, and I'd made arrangements with one of the women at the shop to help me wrap it properly on the morning of the celebration. It was a sari, after all, and it required so much folding and twisting and turning that I would have needed an illustrated manual to figure it out, and even then I probably couldn't have managed. When I arrived home, however, the woman had left a message on our answering machine saying she had been called out of town on family business, and would be unable to help. Back in the store, she had made me look absolutely stunning, and now she was telling me I was on my own. I called Anita straightaway. "I can't believe this is happening; can you do it for me?" I wailed. Even though Anita occasionally wore saris to functions, she didn't feel confident enough to wrap mine on my wedding day.

"There's a woman in Walsall who can do it," she said. "But you'll have to go to her. She won't come to you."

"But that's miles away! I'm supposed to drive there and back on the morning of my wedding? *In* my wedding sari?"

"But I'll drive you out to Walsall in the morning, and I'll get you back in plenty of time for the wedding."

At this point, Kev could hear me wailing on the phone, and he came in to ask me what was wrong. I told him I had to go to Walsall on the morning of the wedding, to deal with "something," and he looked absolutely perplexed. "You can't go to Walsall on the morning of your wedding," he said. "You need to just get your dress on and get yourself to your nan's, ready to be picked up."

I started crying. I didn't want to ruin the surprise by telling him that, no, I couldn't dress myself, because this wasn't just any dress, so I started crying harder. Kev was completely mystified. "What is it?" he said. "I don't understand what's going on."

"I can't tell you," I said.

"Well, if you don't tell me, I can't help you, can I?"

"I can't tell you."

"Why can't you tell me? You are marrying me, we shouldn't have secrets." Obviously this had started to get to him.

"You don't understand!" I said.

"Then tell me," he said.

"It's about my dress. It's not just a dress! It's a sari. I'm wearing a sari!"

His face went slack. He seemed to be fighting shock. "A sari. Yes. Right, now I understand." And with that, he turned on his heels and left the room. I started crying harder. I was thinking, *I'm going to show up at my wedding in my underwear.*

But a few minutes later, Kev was back. He phoned around and found an Asian woman who would be glad to help me out, and she would see that everything went according to plan. He was still in a mild state of shock, though, and I could only imagine what he was thinking. He must have assumed I'd be making my way toward him in a bright red sari and matching scarf, with a bindi painted dead-center on my forehead.

Of course, in the end, I looked quite lovely—if I may so myself. I walked down the aisle to the strains of *Almost There*, by Andy Williams, with my dad and Charlie at my side. We reached Kev and the song ended, right on cue, and the three of us stood there together, hand in hand. Kev choked and sputtered his way through his vows, and I wept through mine. Charlie proudly held the rings. It was very emotional—far more intense and spiritually uplifting than anything I could have expected. As we turned to make our way back down the aisle, a married couple now, I noticed that half the wedding party was in tears. We took our first step and—on cue again—Barry White came blasting over the speakers: *You're the First, the Last, My Everything*. And I just couldn't help myself. I was

Photo © Andrew Thomas

Mom, Dad, and Charlie celebrating on our wedding day

so happy we started dancing in the aisle. And Kev got right into it. Then everyone joined us, and it was a truly magical occasion—one of the most beautiful days of my life. It was everything a wedding should be, and I honestly felt like the luckiest girl in the world.

We had lunch—bangers and mash and cheesecake—and, of course, the speeches. I decided I wanted to throw my bouquet. I know it sounds silly, but it's something I've always dreamed of doing. So I'm gathering up the single women: "Come on, girls! I'm going to throw my bouquet. Let's see who's next." As soon as they were all lined up, I turned my back and threw it high, and then I turned again to see who the lucky girl would be. That's when I noticed Anita's brother, Gopi, off to one side, watching this joyful madness, smoking a cigarette. And then I saw that my bouquet was falling in his direction. Gopi reached up, calm as you please, and effortlessly snatched it out of the air with one hand. Everyone burst into laughter, and Gopi joined in, looking a bit sheepish. But would you believe it? Some time later, Gopi was indeed the next person to marry! Coincidence? I think not.

Kev and I had booked a honeymoon to South Africa, but it wasn't until December 5, so we went home and began our life as a married couple. Between readings, I returned to the doctor for a checkup, and was found to have some precancerous cells. It would require surgery, but the doctor was kind enough to put if off till after the honeymoon.

South Africa was everything we had hoped for and more. We stayed at the home of our friends Chris and Linzi, in Hout Bay, near the beach, not far from Cape Town, and we met some wonderful people, including a woman who worked for a church at a local township. We went to visit one day—this was the real Africa—and she introduced us to a little boy, Zimmy, whose mother was an alcoholic and whose father had unfortunately just died of AIDS. He was undernourished and suffering from TB. We asked if we could help in some way, and it was arranged that we become his sponsor.

The money we donate enables him to have access to medicines, school, and a roof over his head. He recently turned seven, the same age as my Charlie, and now looks a million times better. We sponsor him to this day, but hope that in the future his education will enable him to become self-sufficient.

Two weeks after we flew home, on December 24, 2004, a tsunami struck the Far East, killing 300,000 people. It was the worst natural disaster in recorded history and just as I had said on the ill-fated *Predictors* pilot, the world came together to provide help.

In January, I went to the hospital for my procedure—I had part of my cervix removed—and made a quick recovery. But three weeks later, on a Friday morning, I woke up feeling perfectly awful. I looked up and saw Ben at the foot of my bed. It had been a while since I'd had a visit from my handsome spirit guide, and I asked him where he'd been. "I only come when you need me," he said. "And you need me now."

"I do?"

"Yes," he said. "You have a cyst, and it needs to be removed."

He disappeared as abruptly as he'd arrived, and I immediately booked an appointment with my doctor. I told them it was urgent, and they squeezed me in that day. "I have a cyst that needs to be removed," I told her.

"Are you a doctor?"

"No," I said. "Let's just say I have more information than most."

"What does that mean?"

"You don't want to know," I said.

She examined me and said that something felt a little off, and she sent me home with antibiotics. "I'll be back in a week," I predicted, and I left.

I went back the following Friday, as predicted, feeling considerably worse. The doctor had asked several people questions about me, and had even spoken to a colleague who'd been to see me for a reading, so on this visit she was somewhat more receptive to my medical diagnosis. She sent me to the hospital for a scan and they found a slight abnormality, and while they didn't appear concerned, they decided to keep me for observation.

My spirit guide, Ben, made one of his infrequent appearances. "Lisa," he said. "You have a very high threshold for pain. Other women would be agonizing. So agonize a little."

I decided to let them know how much pain I was in, and on that Sunday, the doctor decided to give me a laparoscopy just to play it safe. While I was on the gurney, being wheeled toward the examining room, one of the nurses recognized me. She trotted alongside the gurney, talking a mile a minute. "Everything you told me has come true!" she said. "You spoke to my father, which was one of the greatest gifts ever, and you told me I'd be working in a hospital—and here I am, working in a hospital!"

Moments later, the anesthesiologist was leaning over me, and the next thing I knew I was waking up in the recovery room. Now it was the doctor who was leaning over me. "Lisa, I don't know how you knew what you knew, but you were right. There was a cyst in there the size of a grapefruit. You were in surgery for three hours."

I went home five days later, completely exhausted but determined to get back to work. Kev had other ideas. He could see I needed time to recuperate, so he canceled two weeks' worth of appointments. With so much time on my hands, I found myself becoming increasingly introspective. Initially, I was angry about my continued medical battles, and I began to feel a little sorry for myself. But before long I snapped out of it. I was alive, after all, and on the mend. And really, what could I do about the past? It was the same with the Tarot cards: past, present and future. Nan had taught me not to pay any attention to the past, since it was unchangeable, and it seemed like a good, all-around life lesson. Some of us hold on to the past with a ferocity that defies logic. The fact is, the past only serves to drag us down. *Today* is what matters. To be present.

To be in the moment. To open our eyes to this vibrant, incredible world around us, seen and unseen. It is all well and good to think about the forces that shaped us, but only today matters. The choices I made today would determine my entire future.

"I have a crazy thought," I told Kev.

"Another one?" he said, smiling.

"I was thinking I should try to put together some kind of development course for my clients."

"Course?"

"A written version of what I did long ago for that group of clients of mine."

"I think that's a great idea; people will love it," he said.

"I know it sounds a little much—who am I to try to teach anybody anything!—but people are always asking me for advice, and I've actually picked up a thing or two in my crazy life."

It was true. I *had* learned a few things. Letting go of the past was only the beginning. I understood the importance of empathy and of compassion. I knew spirit guides and invisible helpers. And I was convinced beyond a shadow of a doubt there was no such thing as a coincidence.

Because of my experiences, I also knew that death wasn't the end. Or I *believed* that, anyway.

I brought my laptop to bed with me and typed my first sentence: *My name is Lisa Williams, and I have a few things I'd like to share with you.*

Kev walked in and looked over at me. "So how's the course going?" he asked, grinning.

"I don't like the first sentence," I said. "But I can always go back and fix it."

Some weeks later, I went to Thailand on a retreat to help me recover. The work on my course was going slowly, but I hoped to learn a few things on this trip that might help, things I could share with others.

The Thailand I saw was an incredibly spiritual country. I felt energized, and healthier than I had in years, and I heard a great deal of talk, from many of the people at the retreat, about past-life regression. On further inquiry, I was told that a very gifted woman lived on the far side of the island where we were staying, and I was urged to call and schedule an appointment.

It was raining hard the day of my appointment. I took a cab from the spa resort where I was staying to the far side of the island, and I was a little nervous. I didn't speak the language, and I didn't know where I was going, and I was relying on a driver with whom I couldn't communicate. But we arrived safely, and I asked the driver to come back for me in three hours.

The house was very modest—almost a hut, in fact—and the woman I was seeing turned out to be an American. When I stepped inside, she looked at me and said, "I've been waiting for you to come. I've been waiting for a long time." She lay me down on a bed and covered me with a blanket. "It is an honor to have you in my home," she said.

I really didn't understand what she meant, and for a while I wondered if perhaps I'd come on the wrong day—that she was expecting someone else.

"I am going to hypnotize you," she said. "Are you familiar with hypnosis?"

"Yes, I am," I said.

"Well, as you know, you're going to remain conscious, but we're going to try to tap into your subconscious, and together we'll see what we find," she explained. "I will keep notes of the session, and you can take them home with you when we're done."

"That sounds great," I said.

She spoke gently, and I felt myself growing heavier, and sinking deeper and deeper into the narrow bed. Before I knew it, I was crying.

"Who are you?" she said.

"My name is Jimmy," I said.

"How old are you?"

"I'm ten years old."

"Are you alone?"

"No, my sister is here. She's blond."

"And your parents?"

"My mother is very sick, and my father is a very mean man. I want to run away from home."

She asked me a few more questions, but I couldn't see everything clearly—I thought I was on a farm in Ireland, for some reason, but I couldn't explain why—and she moved on. Next, I found myself running through a cornfield, as fast as my ten-year-old legs could carry me, and from there I found I'd stowed away aboard a ship. Another little boy, also a stowaway, was with me.

"What year is it?" the woman asked me.

I saw a large tea chest nearby. The date was clearly stamped across one side. "It says 1876," I said. I couldn't believe it was so clear and vivid. I could hear the wind howling, and the crashing of the waves, and I found myself fighting the pitching ship.

I remember reaching into the tea chest, trying to keep my balance, and seeing a collection of silver teaspoons. I took one and put it in my pocket. Just then, I heard a man's voice booming above me. "You, boy!" I looked up, terrified. A large man with a huge gray beard and a tall hat was staring down at me. "Yes, you! How did you get on this ship? And what is that you just stole?"

"N-nothing," I stammered.

"Give it back or I'll throw you overboard."

"I don't have anything," I lied. I don't know why I lied. I was terrified of him, but I wanted to give the silver teaspoon to my mother, as a present. This made absolutely no sense, of course, since I was running away from home.

The man reached for my hair and yanked me to my feet, then dug into my pocket for the silver spoon and tossed me into the water. I was under before I could even scream.

"What happened?" the lady asked.

"I drowned," I said, crying.

"You're safe," she said. "Let's keep going."

I remember thinking, *Now I know why I'm afraid of the ocean.*

In another life, I died in a fire. I was with Kev who was also in my life but his name was different. I wasn't clear on where we were but I knew we were in a building. I always thought it odd that when Kev and I went into a new building, the first thing we did was look for the fire exit; now I knew why! In yet another life I was mauled to death by three Dobermans. I was a little girl, playing in front of a large, opulent-looking house, when the first of three dogs came sniffing around me. The more I tried to shoo it away, the more insistent it became, until it finally bit me. When I screamed out, two more Dobermans, alerted by my cries, came loping into view. That was the last thing I remembered.

Both of those experiences were tremendously significant: I had mentioned them—or parts of them, anyway—to my parents as a child, but back then I'd no idea where they had come from.

The lady now took me to my next life, and before I knew it, I was screaming in pain. "Where are you?" the lady said.

I tried to piece things together. It was 1847. I was in a hospital, but there was something shabby about the place. I was shocked to realized I was about to have a backstreet abortion. "He doesn't want it!" I wailed.

"Who?" the lady asked.

"The father. He doesn't want the baby, and he doesn't want me."

"Who are you?"

"Amanda."

"How old are you?"

"Twenty-six."

"What's happening?"

"I hurt. My stomach hurts. I want to have this baby, but my mom won't let me have it."

The abortion proceeded, but an infection set in and I realized I was dying. When I opened my eyes, I found I was back in the present, on the bed. I was perspiring freely, and I could feel my heart beating wildly. The American woman was looking down at me. "Are you okay?" she said.

"I think so," I said.

"What are you thinking about?"

"I'm thinking about my little boy, Charlie. I was twenty-six when I had him."

"There you go," she said. "You got another life, another chance."

She helped me sit up. "This might sound odd," I said, "but I've had a lot of medical problems—women's problems. I wonder if it's connected to the abortion."

"Everything happens for a reason," she said. "Sometimes, things happen to us because we've carried them over from a past life."

"But not everything we bring is bad?"

"No," she said, smiling. "Look at Mozart. People say he was practicing his scales long before he was born."

I returned from Thailand, convinced that I had passed this way before, and that I'd pass this way again. It seemed to me that every day on earth provided a chance to become a better person, and I promised myself never to forget that.

Photo by Kevin Harris

*Lisa in Toys "R" Us moments before giving a
reading on the largest indoor Ferris wheel*

chapter 10

America

By the middle of 2005, I was working as hard as I'd ever worked in my life. I was doing four readings a day, five days a week, and people were being forced to book several months in advance. I couldn't handle it—I couldn't bear to disappoint people—so Kev was managing every aspect of my career. I wouldn't even pick up the phone because people would just expect me to read for them there and then.

"I feel like an air-traffic controller, " Kev remarked. "You have four today and you're going to Stratford-upon-Avon tomorrow for a party of five."

That was another thing I'd gotten into: private parties.

One Friday in late June, I went off to one such party. I wasn't feeling terribly well, but the hostess was a regular client and I didn't want to disappoint her. I did her reading first, and her late husband appeared to me. "You're not very well," he said.

I turned to her and said, "You're not very well."

"What on earth does he mean?" she said. "I feel fine."

"Not her," the husband corrected himself. "It's *you* that's not well."

"Me?"

"Yes. You need to go home and look after yourself."

Suddenly, I felt hot and clammy, as if I was on the verge of throwing up. I excused myself and went to the bathroom, and I felt so lightheaded that I sat on the cold stone floor. The next thing I knew, I was hearing the voice of the hostess: "Lisa? Lisa, are you okay in there?"

My head hurt. I realized I had passed out and struck my head against the radiator. I managed to get to my feet and opened the door. "Lisa!" she said. "You look ill. Are you all right? I heard a horrible thud. Are you hurt?"

"I'm okay," I said. "I'll just call my husband and have him pick me up."

But she wouldn't hear of it. She had me lay on her bed and rang Kev, and handed me the phone. I was feeling really awful—it was my lower abdomen again—and I thought that at any moment I might black out. When I heard Kev's voice, I told him I was sick and asked him to fetch me straightaway. "No," he said. "Have the woman order an ambulance, and get yourself to the hospital."

Kev met me at the hospital, and by the time I arrived I was feeling even worse. As we waited for the doctor, I reached for his hands and placed them against my belly. I could literally feel the pain dissipating. The healing energy was running through my hands, into Kev's hands, and back into me. A few moments later, I drifted off.

When I awoke, I looked over and found Kev slumped over in his chair. "Kev?" I called out. "Kev?"

He opened his eyes, confused, and looked around as if to get his bearings.

"You okay?" I said.

"I'm exhausted," he said. "I've never felt so drained in my life."

"It's the healing," I said. "I used your energy to help me. It can really take it out of you if you don't know what you are doing, but thank you."

The doctor came in with bad news: I needed a hysterectomy. I looked over at Kev, fighting tears. We hadn't been married long, and I had so much hoped to have a child with him. I had always known the chances were slim, but you always hold on to that one small hope. The doctor left and it was just Kev and me again. "I'm sorry," I said.

"What are you apologizing for?" Kev said. "There's only one thing I care about, and that's seeing you get well."

The surgery was scheduled for November 17, 2005, nearly five months away.

I went home with megadoses of antibiotics, and got back to work. Within a week I was feeling better. Kev had some work to do on the Watermarque apartment, and since I was feeling better he went ahead and scheduled it. The workmen would be arriving very early in the morning, so he planned to spend the night there. I made plans to have my friend Kirsten come by for a glass of wine, and Kev left shortly after she arrived.

At about eight o'clock, I left Kirsten alone in the lounge for a few minutes and went to put Charlie to bed. I had no sooner returned to the lounge when Charlie appeared at the top of the stairs. "Mummy, can I sleep in your bed tonight?" he said. He knew Kev would be away for the night, and he wanted to be close to me, and since I'm a real soft touch, I gave in. "Sure you can, darling," I said. I went up and got him tucked in, and again returned to the lounge.

"Would you like me to do a reading for you?" I asked Kirsten.

"I'd love it," she said. "You haven't read for me in a very long time."

It was true. She had once been a client but had become a good friend, and I tend not to like reading for friends. I'm involved in their lives, so I worry about what I might see.

We went over to my reading table, I reached for my cards, and I read for her. We discussed various aspects of her life, but it wasn't a standout reading, probably because I was being overcautious. I tidied up the Tarot cards and set them aside, and Kirsten looked at her watch and realized it was time to go. At that instant, I heard a scream that no mother ever wants to hear. It was Charlie. I ran up the stairs with the hairs standing up on the back of my neck, and I rushed into our room. Charlie was sitting up in bed, eyes wide, fixated on something just above the window frame. I looked over and saw the blackest shadow I'd ever seen in my life—a shadow so substantial it seemed made of black silk—I grabbed Charlie and lifted him out of the bed. For a moment, I couldn't move—and I couldn't take my eyes off the shadow. It looked like a man with a big pointy hat, and I could see a long, gnarled finger, curved like a scythe. As I turned toward the door, the shadow disappeared. Charlie was shaking in my arms, still crying, so I reached over and flicked on the light. "Look, Charlie," I said. "It's gone. There's nothing there."

He buried his face against my shoulder, wailing, not wanting to look, so I carried him downstairs. Kirsten was standing in the lounge, looking over at us, mute and white with fear. "What happened?" I said. "Did you see something?"

It took her a moment to compose herself. "This thing. I don't know what it was, but just after you went upstairs, this sort of whirly black thing came spinning down the stairs and spun around and shot off into the kitchen."

I was baffled. Still holding Charlie, I went to get my protective crystals—one is clear quartz, the other is an amethyst—and then the three of us went around the house switching on all the lights. I asked the spirits for protection for the house and everybody in it, and Charlie eventually calmed down. Just then, it happened again: This black shadow shot past us, twisting like a scarf in the wind, and disappeared toward the rear of the house. I grabbed my purse and my keys. "You know what?" I said. "We're out of here!" I led Kirsten outside, waited until she pulled away, then strapped Charlie into his car seat and took off. I was wearing my slippers and an old sweat suit, and Charlie was in a pair of pajamas that were too small for him.

I rang Kev, but it was late, and he always turns his mobile off at night.

"Where are we going, Mummy?" Charlie asked.

"We are going on an adventure," I said.

"What was that thing?"

"It's nothing to worry about, sweetheart, it was just a shadow."

I thought we might check into a hotel, but then I decided we'd drive to Kev's and wake him. We finally got there and I buzzed repeatedly, and just as I was about to despair, another tenant arrived home and let us though. I pounded on the door to Kev's apartment and a few moments later I could hear him stumbling around inside. He opened the door, looking sleepy and startled. "W-what's going on?" he said. "What are you doing here?" We went inside, I told him the story, and the three of us spent the night in the apartment—with all of the lights on.

In the morning, the workmen arrived, and I told Kev I had to go back to the house for a scheduled reading. I was sure things at home would be fine, but I dropped Charlie at my mother's just in case.

I walked into the house. The lights were still on, and everything looked to be just as I had left it. But then I crossed over to my reading table and saw that the Tarot cards had been scattered across the floor. I distinctly remembered stacking them together into a single pile, right after doing Kirsten's reading. This is what I always did; I treated my cards with respect.

Kev arrived a short time later; we went up to the bedroom and I closed my eyes and asked the spirits to help me get rid of this evil presence. A man's voice responded: "I'm not talking while he's in the room."

I told Kev what the man had said.

"Is it the shadow?" he asked, looking around the room.

"It seems to be," I said.

Kev went outside and sat at the top of the stairs, listening.

"Who are you and why are you here?" I asked the spirit.

"My name is Jimmy. I'm trying to get your attention."

"You have it," I said. "You didn't have to go through Charlie to get to me."

"But that's the way I do it."

"Well, I don't like it," I said. "What do you want from me?"

"I think you can help me."

"With what?" I asked. "And why me?"

Instead of answering, he suddenly appeared again, hanging from the ceiling. He was more substantial than he'd been the previous night. I could make out a pair of big, bulging eyes, set against his paper-white face. For some reason, I wasn't afraid. We were talking, and that took the edge off.

"What are you hanging from up there for?" I said. "You look like Dracula."

"That's what they used to call me," he said.

"Who?"

"Everyone."

"What happened to you?" I asked.

"I killed myself in prison."

"What were you in prison for?"

"Sexual assault. I assaulted two young girls." He told me about the girls, including their names and about the horrible shame he felt to that day, then said he was afraid to cross over because of this terrible thing he'd done. "My parents are both in spirit, and I don't think they will accept me."

When he fell silent, I asked the spirits to help him cross over and encouraged him to go. After a while I didn't hear him anymore and the house became very still and calm.

He was gone.

I went back to my mother's to get Charlie. On the drive home he asked about the shadow, and I told him it was gone, never to return, and I knew it to be true.

The next day was a Sunday, and I seldom do readings on Sunday, but my friend Margaret needed a little help, so I made an exception. Margaret was one of the women who had trained with me a few years earlier, and I told her about the experience with Dracula. She listened, wide-eyed, and left the house looking shaken, and an hour later she rang me. "Lisa, I have something to tell you," she said. "When you mentioned the name 'Dracula,' it struck a chord. I have a cousin we used to call Dracula, on account of his queer looks, but he was a troubled man, and the family lost touch with him many years ago. He was in prison for sexually assaulting two girls." I asked her for the names of the girls and was shocked to hear they were the same names that I was given the night before. Margaret had unwittingly brought him into our home.

I believe I helped Dracula pass over, because I never saw or heard from him again, but his visit convinced me to stop doing readings at home. The following month, Kev and I found a cozy little office in Studley, Warwickshire, two miles from the house, and from that day forth I met most of my clients there.

Shortly after I got settled in, Kev began talking about finding a bigger house for us, and in the weeks ahead we started to browse the estate agents. But we did so halfheartedly, since both of us were still wondering if anything was going to happen for us in America.

I had another bizarre experience around the same time, as frightening as my encounter with Dracula, if in a completely different way. A friend of Kev's had asked me to come to a party to do a series of readings, and we booked it for a Thursday night. By nine o'clock, I'd done five readings—party readings run shorter than regular readings—and I was exhausted. I wanted go home, but there was one woman among the guests who insisted on having a reading. I had noticed her earlier because she seemed somehow deeply wounded, and the other guests seemed to be keeping her at arm's length, but suddenly she'd become aggressive. I was a little put out, but I agreed to do her reading, and we got started. Almost immediately, I discovered that she had tried to take her own life not three weeks prior. I suddenly felt enormously tired, and depressed as well, but I didn't want to quit in the middle of a reading, so I saw it through to the end. I could hardly keep my eyes open on the ride home, and for some inexplicable reason I felt that at any moment I would burst into tears.

When I came though the front door, Kev was in the lounge, reading, and Charlie was already fast asleep. I told Kev I was exhausted, kissed him good-night, and went up to bed, and I didn't move a muscle till morning. When I opened my eyes, I felt awful. It was Friday, and it was my morning to get Charlie ready for school—Kev and I take turns—but I simply couldn't get myself out of bed. I tried, but my limbs felt so heavy I could hardly move them. "Kev," I said. "I don't feel great. Would you please take Charlie to school for me today?"

"If you get him dressed and feed him, I'll take him," he said.

That wasn't exactly what I wanted to hear, and I became really angry—and please understand, I rarely get angry. "What's the point of that, then?" I snapped.

Kev rolled over in bed and looked at me, and I started to cry and he told me to stop being silly. He must have put it down to hormones. Bad as I was feeling, I managed to drag myself out of bed. I got Charlie dressed and fed, and drove him to school myself. I'd kept my foul mood in check throughout, but on the drive back I felt like jumping out of my skin. When I got home, Kev was in the kitchen, calm as can be, and the bile just spilled out of me. "I can't believe you wouldn't do that one little thing for me," I snapped, practically hissing with rage. "You selfish bastard." I proceeded to call him every ugly name under the sun, then stormed upstairs and screamed my lungs out. I was behaving like a demonic three-year-old who wasn't getting her way—fists clenched, teeth clenched—and I couldn't for the life of me understand where this was coming from.

After a few minutes, with the tantrum somewhat under control, I grabbed my appointments diary and began calling all the clients who were scheduled for that day, canceling my readings. After making the last call, I flung my phone against the wall. The battery flew one way and the Sim card flew another. I started screaming again, "I hate my work! I hate my job! I hate my life! These dead people are driving me insane!"

I honestly *felt* insane. I stormed back into the kitchen and found Kev making me a drink. "I don't know what's wrong with you," he said.

"Neither do I!" I snapped.

Suddenly I dropped into a fetal position on the kitchen floor and began to keen and wail like an injured animal. Kev had no idea what do to. He must have thought I'd turned into a complete nutter. But slowly, patiently, he managed to calm me down, and when I'd returned to some semblance of normalcy he suggested we go for a walk.

I slipped into my coat, grabbed my hat, and literally jammed it onto my head. Kev walked me outside, put me in the car, and drove us out to the nearby lake. We started walking around the lake, but I began crying again. I didn't know what I was crying about, and I didn't know how to control it.

"Do you want to tell me what's wrong?" he asked.

"I don't know what's wrong!"

"Surely you must have some idea?"

"I don't! I don't! I don't!"

"You want me to take you somewhere nice for lunch?"

"No. I don't want to be around people."

"So what do you want to do?"

"I know," I said after a pause. "I know what I need to do."

There was a little shop in the area that sold crystals and witchy things, and I felt literally compelled to go see it. Kev took me. It was fifteen minutes away, and I felt better with every passing minute. I felt as if somehow I would find the answer in that store.

I hadn't been in the store for half a moment when the girl behind the counter took a look at me and said, "It's a good thing you've got your hat on today, because you're under psychic attack."

"I'm what?" I said, taken aback.

"Have you felt weird today?"

"Weird? That's an understatement!"

"I could see right off that you've been under psychic attack," she said. She went on to explain that a psychic attack is an assault on one's aura, and that the attack was probably not deliberate. "Sometimes we just cross paths with the wrong person," she said. "And we feel as if we're being attacked on every side."

"You're absolutely right!" I said.

I thought back to the woman at the party, the one who had survived a suicide attempt, and wondered if she had anything to do with it, albeit unwittingly.

The girl in the store disappeared into the bookshelves and returned with a book for me. It was called *Dancing with the Devil*, and it was written by David Ashworth. "Here," she said. "Read this. I think you'll find it very helpful."

After I flipped though the book, I knew exactly what to do. I placed stones all over the house—amethyst, tourmaline, clear quartz—and then burned sage throughout the house and left fresh sage in every nook and cranny. Then I went upstairs and took a bath in sea salt and bicarbonate of soda. I had read that this would cleanse my aura, and it seemed to work.

"That was weird," Kev said.

"You know what's even weirder? Before we left, when I jammed my hat onto my head—I was operating on pure instinct. I was blocking unwelcome visitors. It's like putting up a sign for the spirits: DO NOT DISTURB."

"I have no idea what you're talking about," Kev said. Although I could pretty much switch my gift on and off, covering my head seemed to protect me further.

A few week later, Kev and Charlie and I went off to Leeds for a weekend to visit Chris and Linzi. Late Saturday, I used the computer to check my e-mail, and there was a note from someone called Ray Brune, whom I didn't know. The subject line read: Merv Griffin. I learned that Ray and his partner, Andrew Yani, were Emmy-winning producers, who had just started working with Merv, and who had viewed *The Predictors*. Of the five panelists on the pilot, Ray wrote, there was only one they really wanted to work with—and that would be lucky me. Was I interested? I was gobsmacked. At that point, I'd pretty much forgotten about America, so it was nice to see that America hadn't forgotten about me. I shot back a quick e-mail: "Yes, I'm interested. We're away at the moment, but we will be back Sunday night—let's speak Monday." I left my number.

When we connected, Ray wasted no time: "Merv loves you, and so do we. We love the energy you create, and we want to do a pilot with you. We were thinking of something like 'A Day in the Life of Lisa Williams.'"

"That sounds great," I said.

"Wonderful," he said. "Let me talk to Merv, and to my partner, and we'll be in touch." We didn't think anything more about it, as we knew from experience that it could be another year before we heard anything else. But we were wrong. Next thing I knew, rough drafts of the show were being e-mailed over, and we started discussing the best way to film me demonstrating my skills.

Six weeks later, Kev and I left Charlie with my mom and jetted off to New York. Ray and Andrew booked us into a hotel near Times Square, and they arrived shortly after we did to take us to dinner. I was wearing my DO NOT DISTURB hat, and I told Ray the story behind it. He was keenly interested, but I could see that Andrew wasn't buying any of it—he was a complete nonbeliever.

Kev turned to him and said, "You just wait. She will have changed your mind by the end of the week."

It was raining heavily and we joked about us bringing the English weather with us. We had a lovely evening, chatting and getting to know each other, and the next morning, at ten, they showed up with a camera crew and we walked into Times Square. They said we would pick people at random, and that I'd talk to them, and we'd see what developed, if anything. It was still pouring when we left the hotel, and raining harder when we reached Times Square, but there were plenty of people around, unfazed by the bad weather. The first man I spoke to turned out to be a tourist from Australia. I walked up to him and said, "I need to give you a name: Christopher."

"My grandfather's name was Christopher," he said.

"And who's Mary? That's your grandmother, isn't it?"

"Whoa!" he said. "How did you do that?"

Man-on-the-street readings in New York City

And I said, "They're telling me that you used to play the piano and sing, but very badly."

"How can you possibly know that?!" he said.

"It's my job," I said.

After we left, Andrew was shaking his head in disbelief. "Holy shit," he said, and he kept repeating it. "Holy shit!" Ray was thrilled, and Kev was just gloating: *That's my girl!*

I talked to a young woman who had lost a school friend in an accident, and to a father who was estranged from his son, and then I went into Toys 'R' Us, the largest toy store I'd ever seen in my life, and joined an unsuspecting woman on the indoor Ferris wheel. When I told her who I was, and why the cameras were rolling, she was elated. She was from out of town, she said, and she had promised herself to visit a psychic while in New York. "And suddenly, out of nowhere, you appear," she said. "What a wonderful coincidence!"

"There are no coincidences," I said.

The next day, Ray and Andrew came to fetch us in a van and we headed into the southern part of Manhattan. I had no idea where we were going, and even though I kept asking, they told me that they wanted to see what I could pick up. A short way into the ride, I had a feeling we were getting close, and I told Ray. He looked over at Andrew, then back at me, and nodded. "You're right," he said. "We're very close."

The cameraman started filming me.

"I have a young girl with me," I said. "She keeps saying the name 'Peter.' She says this is going to be very hard for me but she will help me." I felt this overwhelming urge to cry, but I fought it back. I continued to tell everyone in the van what I was picking up as it came to me, feeling more and more upset. And then I started sobbing. I couldn't help it. Even though I had these strangers listening to me and a camera shoved in my face, I couldn't stop crying. I looked at the camera, put my hand up, and said, "I can't do this, I can't do this, turn it off. . . . Please!"

I looked up to find that we were across the street from Ground Zero. We parked and the crew got out, leaving me to pull myself together. And finally when I felt able, Kev wrapped his arms around me and we went to have a closer look at the site. It was enormous. I had never imagined it was so big. Suddenly, the little girl was back. "Come on," she said. "I'm going to show you where Peter is."

I followed her and found myself at a spot commemorating the dead, and listing all of their names. I saw the name Peter Adamson, and turned to look for the little girl, but she was gone. Then a man's voice rang in my head, clear as a bell: "My wife was pregnant when I died. We have a little girl now. Going to be four years old. She's a beautiful girl. I wish I could have been there for her." I relayed everything that I was getting for the camera. It had been a very hard day already, but we went off to investigate some hauntings at Grand Central Station before calling it a day.

The next day, we met Ray and Andrew in the lobby again and the van was waiting for us outside. As we piled inside, they told us we were leaving the city to have a look at a haunted house. We drove out to Long Island in the rain, to a huge, sprawling, dilapidated estate that I later learned was on the market for many millions of dollars. As we pulled up, I saw a woman waiting for us by the open front door. We hurried through the pounding rain and took shelter under the parapet. The woman's name was Monica, and she was a local historian who knew absolutely everything about the house. She was very open to the psychic world and agreed to help us on a "ghost hunt." (The owners of the house were actually sitting downstairs, and I later learned they were under the impression that we were there to shoot a segment for an antiques show!)

The moment we stepped inside, I sensed that the place was absolutely overflowing with spirits. In one direction I could hear a young girl crying, I saw an old man limp across the foyer, and from a bedroom upstairs I heard the awful screams of a woman.

I was drawn to the west wing, to a room that had fallen into disrepair. It was empty, but I sensed that it had once been the master bedroom. Monica and the camera crew were right behind me. There was a gold antique bed canopy standing alone in the corner of the empty room. I went over and placed my hands on it. "I keep feeling that this belongs to the monarchy and I'm seeing a capital *M* attached, though I am not sure what that means. But it has a French connection," I said. "This belongs to the rightful owner of this house. And the gentleman concerned had a limp and also a problem with his left ear."

Monica's jaw dropped. "Oh my God! You can't possibly know that! You're freaking me out! I need a Valium."

As it turned out, the bed canopy had once belonged to Napoleon Bonaparte, and it had been purchased and shipped over from France by the original owner of the house, F.W. Woolworth, the department store magnate. Monica then told us that F.W. Woolworth had long believed that he was, in fact, Napoleon reincarnated. As for the capital *M*, Monica said I was probably referring to the Château de Malmaison, where Napoleon lived with Josephine for a time.

We drove back to Manhattan that afternoon, and for the next few days, I did readings for people who had been picked at random by the producers. I was in mid-reading for a gentleman, when suddenly a young man dressed in motorbike gear appeared. I described him to my client, but he couldn't relate. And then Andrew, the non-believer—well, actually, he was a little more open to the spirit world since the Woolworth Mansion experience—suddenly turned to me and said, "Actually, I think this message is for me."

I turned my attention to Andrew. "He is telling me that he died in a motorcycle accident; the throttle was stuck open. He tells you he is sorry and he should have listened. But he just wanted to say good-bye."

Andrew went pale. He had not mentioned this to anyone, but he had gotten a call the day before, informing him that his friend had died in a motorcycle accident in LA. The call came from a mutual friend, Matt, who had ridden the same bike the morning of the accident and had told his friend he shouldn't take it out until he got it fixed. Sadly he didn't listen and died that afternoon. Shaken, Andrew left the room.

All in all, the trip was deemed a huge success. Ray and Andrew said they would send me a copy of the presentation tape as soon as it was ready, and we said our good-byes.

Kev and I flew home, and I had my hysterectomy on November 17. After the op, the hot flashes started and menopause kicked in, but I could cope with this; what I couldn't deal with was my little boy asking me if I was going to die everytime I was in the hospital. I kept reassuring Charlie that I was going to be all right, but death was clearly on his mind. Ironically, during this very period I got a call from a young woman who was herself facing death. Her name was Mel. She was twenty-four years old and had just been diagnosed with ovarian cancer, and my heart went out to her because I'd been the same age when I was first diagnosed.

Mel had stage four cancer and the doctors had given her only a thirty percent chance of surviving. She wanted to do all that she could to heal herself and asked if I would give her healing. Having been in her situation, I wanted to help, and I spoke with Kev about it because I knew it would be intense and would have an impact on our family life. As ever, he was totally supportive and I remember him telling me that I was put on the earth to help and to do all I could.

I agreed to see Mel every other day and told her that the healing I gave would be in addition to the doctor's normal treatments. Two days later, she came over to the house. She was petite, with long blond hair and a beautiful, smiling face. I sat her down and told her I needed to know what the doctors had said. She described everything from the extent of the chemo that she was going to receive to the operations that she was facing, and not once did the smile leave her face. "Lisa, I am going to get through this, I am not going to let this thing beat me!"

Her positivity was incredible, and I knew this would help her survive.

For the next six weeks I rearranged my schedule and saw Mel every other day. I would place crystals on the major energy points of her body, which are called the chakras, and I placed my hands on those parts of her body where she was feeling the most pain. She started chemo and radiation therapy and continued her healing treatments with me.

Around this time, we had an e-mail from LA, with the presentation video attached. Kev and I huddled in the kitchen in front of the computer and watched it—and I was completely blown away. I couldn't believe that was *me* on television. "She looks like an impostor," I told Kev. "I don't even know that woman." We laughed.

I called Ray and Andrew after we'd watched it through twice.

"So you liked it?" Ray said.

"Liked it?" I said. "I *loved* it."

"Well, we still need to sell it to the networks," he said. "It would be great to have you in the room with us. Could you manage a few days in LA?"

"Oh, I think I can manage that," I said. I was acting very cool, but inside I was bursting with excitement.

While I waited for word on the pitch meetings, I continued to see Mel every other day. She had gone through an intensive chemo regime and the doctors still were not convinced of any progress, but the ever positive Mel kept on going. She had to go into the hospital to have radiation rods placed in her for twenty-four hours to conclude her therapy. As soon as they were removed, Mel called.

She was so excited I could hardly catch her words. "You'll never believe it. When I woke from the operation the doctors told me that eighty percent of my cancer is gone!"

I couldn't believe what I was hearing. "The doctor said that he had never seen such a dramatic improvement and told me that he didn't want to believe in the healing that you were doing, but it must have been working. Lisa, you are healing me!" She began to cry. This was the first time I had ever heard Mel cry. I was so happy for her, and I also felt better about taking my trip to LA.

Two weeks later, I jetted off to Los Angeles. Charlie stayed behind with Kev, and I promised I'd call them every day.

When I arrived at the airport, I was whisked off to a hotel, and the next morning, I went off with Andrew, Ray, and Mark Itkin from the William Morris Agency to meet with the first of the networks. We had meetings lined up all week, and to me they all seemed to go very well. The executives viewed the presentation tape in silence, and praised it generously when it was over, but later Ray told me that film and TV executives were always very positive, which made them impossible to judge.

On the third day of meetings we went to Lifetime to meet with Jessica Samet, one of the top executives. When we arrived, however, something had come up, and Jessica wasn't there, so we met instead with another executive, David Hillman. We played the presentation tape for him, as we had done in our previous meetings, and I watched him watching it, and when a photograph of Peter Adamson appeared on the screen he shouted, "I know that guy! My best friend was his roommate in college!"

"Whoa, what a coincidence," Andrew said.

"There are no coincidences," I said. "David, can I ask you a question? Peter told me that his wife had a little girl he had never met—he had passed over before she was born. We didn't put that in the presentation tape because we were unable to verify it, but it's been playing on my mind."

David was clearly shocked, and looked at me with amazement. "Well, I can tell you that his wife was pregnant when Peter died and that she gave birth to a baby girl a few months after his funeral."

"Did he also have a little sister who died young?" I asked. "Because there was a little girl at the site who led me to him."

"I don't know," he said. "But I know about the baby." He was shaking his head. "I can't believe this. What are the odds? Three thousand people died at the World Trade Center, and we're three thousand miles away, and you walk into my office with a story about a guy I know. Unbelievable."

Later that day, Andrew called to say that David Hillman had spoken to Jessica Samet about the presentation tape, and that she was eager to see it. She had pushed all of her morning meetings and was hoping we could return to Lifetime the following morning at 9 a.m. When we arrived, David led us into Jessica's office and made the introductions. Jessica seemed genuinely excited about the show, but I didn't want to read too much into it.

I suddenly felt someone was trying to get a message to her, so I politely asked her if she would mind if I passed along the message. She was open to hear what I had to say, and in front of everyone, I gave her a mini-reading. She didn't say anything, she just sat there listening to what I was saying, with tears in her eyes. Once I had finished she smiled and thanked me. "You do not now how much that means to me," she said. I always appreciate when people tell me that.

I went back to the hotel, called Kev, spoke to Charlie, and then did a little shopping. As it was my last night, I had arranged to meet Andrew for dinner. When I arrived at the restaurant, he was waiting for me with a bottle of champagne.

"Congratulations," he said, smiling broadly. "Lifetime just bought your show."

Photo by Dana Bordsden

My search for clients on the show

Epilogue

Lifetime bought the show!"

I was in the restaurant bathroom, calling home, bursting to share the good news with Kev. It was Silly o'Clock in Redditch, and I hoped he wouldn't mind. "Are you awake? Did you hear me? They bought the show!"

"Oh my God!" he said.

"I know! I know!"

I flew home the next morning, so excited, and still trying to process what had just happened. Kev and Charlie met me at Heathrow Airport, and it was a tearful reunion. I don't know why, really. I'd only been gone for a week. But it was nice to be back with my boys!

For the next few weeks, we heard nothing, and I began to wonder if the show was actually going to happen. After all, we'd heard plenty of stories about Hollywood. The town was flaky. People made promises they didn't keep. People changed their minds every day, sometimes twice a day. "We have to have a backup plan," I told Kev. "The show might never happen, so it makes no sense to put our lives on hold."

Determined to move forward, we continued house hunting, and we finally found a place we both quite liked, not far from our own house. It had an extra bedroom for visitors, and a big but unkept garden that Kev was just dying to transform. Strangely, I had a feeling we'd never live in it, but we made an offer and put our own place on the market.

I continued to give Mel healing once a week, and she continued to be treated by her regular doctors. She was scheduled to have a scan in a few weeks to see if the chemo and radiation had worked. During those two weeks, the phone calls regarding the show began in earnest. Every time the phone rang after nine o'clock at night, we knew America was calling. It was either Ray or Andrew, with news about the show. "Lisa, it's really happening. Honest."

One night, Merv himself rang. "Lisa," he said in his husky voice. "You're a star. I'm so proud of you. You have such an amazing talent and we're going to make a hit show together. You'll see."

The phone calls became more frequent, until finally one day Ray called with real news. "Lifetime has decided to fast-track the show," he said.

"Great," I replied, not understanding.

Usually, the network orders a pilot, and they make a decision to go to series based on the results, but they were so keen on the show they ordered six episodes in advance—and they had already scheduled them for the fall. (Just to clarify, the presentation tape we'd shot in New York was really made as a selling tool. It had been shot to open the door, not to be put on the air, and it had done its job.)

By this time, we had negotiated the sale of our house, and Kev had been going back and forth with the owners of the new place, trying to get the deal done. Finally, our offer was accepted, and Kev and I didn't know whether to celebrate or to cry.

"I told you I thought we'd never live in it," I said.

Kev shrugged. "If nothing else, it's a good investment."

A week after we exchanged contracts on the house, Ray called. The show was moving forward, and Lifetime had hired Bruce Toms to run it. When I got off the phone, I was excited, but I had a feeling that Bruce Toms was the wrong guy, and I shared it with Kev. "You haven't even met the man," he said.

"I know," I said. "It's just a feeling. I'm sure he's a perfectly nice man, but it just feels wrong."

I planned a trip to LA for a week to help with the show and was leaving the day Mel was going to the hospital to have her scan. Eager to find out the results, I texted her from the airport, asking her to let me know the minute she had the results. I started to board the plane, and my phone rang; it was Mel.

"It's gone, the cancer has gone!" Oh my God! I couldn't believe it. "Thank you, thank you so much," she said. This was the second time I had heard her cry, and this time I was crying with her.

I flew to Los Angeles, rented a car at the airport, and—without even looking at a map—found my way to the Beverly Hilton Hotel. I got there at two o'clock, and immediately went off to West Hollywood to look at the house the producers were thinking of renting for Kev, Charlie, and me. The house was very dark, and it was surrounded by tall hedges that only served to make it more oppressive. Plus it had a musky smell. The only nice part was the big back garden, which I knew Kev would love. As soon as I finished touring the house, I was on my way to a five o'clock meeting with Ray and Andrew.

"Who are we meeting with, then?" I asked. "I wasn't told about any meeting."

"You'll see," Ray said.

When we pulled up in front of the Ritz-Carlton in Marina Del Rey I thought, *This is very posh indeed!* But the meeting apparently wasn't in the hotel. We went past the lobby and through a rear exit and made our way along the marina, past row upon row of yachts, one more impressive than the next.

"Who are we meeting, then?" I asked again.

Andrew gestured like a game-show host and I found myself looking at the most spectacular yacht I'd ever seen. It was called *The*

Griff, and it belonged, of course, to Merv Griffin himself. It wasn't a yacht, really. It was a bloody ship. And standing at the stern, smoking a cigarette, was Merv—smiling and waving at us.

We took our shoes off at the bottom of the stairs and were escorted into Merv's palatial quarters, and I do mean *palatial*. There was a screening room to one side, and the main area consisted of a lounge, a baby grand piano, and a formal dining room—and that was just the part I could *see*. Merv appeared and hurried over in his socks. "Lisa, Lisa, Lisa!" he said, giving me a big hug. "Welcome aboard. It is so nice to see you!"

We had dinner on the deck, within view of the Ritz-Carlton, and I felt like I was in the middle of a fairy tale. *If my friends could see me now!* I thought.

At one point, I heard the distant ringing of a phone, and a moment later one of Merv's deckhands appeared and whispered in his boss's ear. Merv said he'd take the call, and the phone was brought to the table. He apologized to us for the interruption and plunged into conversation, and Ray and Andrew and I tried to carry on without eavesdropping. At one point, though, I distinctly heard him say, "No. She's right here, having dinner with me. Why don't you tell her yourself?" I looked up, and Merv was handing me the phone. "Nancy wants to talk to you," he said.

"Nancy?"

"Nancy Reagan."

The wife of the former president wanted to talk to me?

I took the phone. "Hello?" I said.

And I heard the sweetest, gentlest voice: "Hi, Lisa. It's so nice to speak to you."

"It's nice to speak to you, ma'am." I was trying to compose myself.

"Merv showed me the presentation tape you made, and you are amazing."

Wow! That was so weird. I couldn't believe it. Nancy Reagan

had watched my show, and we were chatting on the phone like old friends!

When I handed the phone back to Merv, I was still completely gobsmacked. "That was Nancy Reagan," I hissed at Ray and Andrew, belaboring the obvious. "Nancy Reagan was talking to little me!"

"Welcome to your new life," Ray said.

The next day I met Bruce Toms, the show-runner, and Bob, the producer, and we all went off to have a drink at the Roosevelt Hotel, on Hollywood Boulevard. It is a landmark, and rife with Hollywood history, and I believe this was where the very first Academy Awards were held.

We had no sooner taken our seats when I saw Marilyn Monroe swan down the stairs and glide across the lobby, toward the exit. She was wearing her famous, or infamous, white dress. My jaw dropped.

"Is something wrong?" Bruce asked me.

"I've just seen Marilyn Monroe."

Nobody said anything. What could they say? I don't think they believed it, and I wasn't sure I believed it either. Maybe I had simply *wanted* to see Marilyn Monroe. I was in Hollywood, after all, and only yesterday I'd been on the phone with Nancy Reagan.

But when the waiter came by to take our order, I couldn't resist. "Excuse me," I said. "I don't know if you believe in this stuff, but I think I just saw Marilyn Monroe."

"Well, I don't know if I believe in that stuff either," he said, "and I've never seen her myself, but you wouldn't be the first person to report it." He turned and indicated the top of the stairs. "In fact, just up there, beyond the wall, there's a mirror that Miss Monroe donated to the hotel. You can have a look at it if you like."

We went and had a look. It was a full-length mirror, and there was an embossed plaque on the wall next to it, explaining that it had been a gift to the hotel from Miss Monroe herself. *Wow*, I thought. *I love this place!*

After two more days of meetings, I flew back to London to plan the future. We were supposed to return to Los Angeles on August 4, which was perfect, since Charlie got out of school in mid-July, and we were expected to spend six weeks there, shooting the six episodes, back to back. We were also expected to live in that musky, oppressive house in West Hollywood, but I really didn't think I had much to complain about. We couldn't wait.

Meanwhile, our house sold, and we closed on the new place, and on August 1 we made the big move into our new place, although we were leaving a scant three days later. And indeed, by August 5 we were living in West Hollywood—the place had been cleaned up, the hedges had been cut back, and the dank smell was almost gone.

We were supposed to start filming the following week, but I had a feeling something was wrong, and I mentioned it to Kevin. Not twenty-four hours later, Ray and Andrew called to tell me that Bruce had resigned over creative differences, but not to worry— they were already talking to someone else.

"What's his name?" I asked.

"Yann DeBonne," Ray said.

"I like him," I said. "He's our guy."

"Good," Andrew said, "because we actually just hired him."

Filming was delayed, of course, so it was clear we'd never return home September 10, as planned. One evening Kev and I found ourselves sitting in the back yard with a glass of wine, wondering what we were going to do. We had Charlie to think about, who would most certainly be missing school, and we had a new house in Redditch that was serving as little more than a storage facility.

I went off to film the show, and it went swimmingly, and before we'd even shot the final episode, Kev and I knew we didn't want to leave LA. We had no idea if Lifetime wanted to pick it up for a second season, so we found ourselves in limbo. As soon as we made

Photo by Kevin Harris

*Lisa with executive producer Yann DeBonne
and good friend Frankie Leigh*

the decision to stay, we found a condo in Beverly Hills, got Charlie enrolled in the neighborhood school, and began to try to figure out what to do about the house in Redditch.

One morning, Dallas, who worked for Merv, was driving me to the office, and he told me, "You do know that your life is about to change in a very big way, don't you?"

"No, it won't," I said. "I'll go back to doing my twenty readings a week. The only difference is that I'll be reading in America."

Dallas just smiled.

We stopped at Jamba Juice for my usual Strawberry Nirvana, and the clerk lit up when she saw me. "You're Lisa Williams!" she said.

"I am," I said, taken aback. It sounded like I was asking a question.

"I saw the promos for your show. I can't wait for it to air!"

From then on, everywhere I went, people came over to say hello.

At Longs Drug Store. At Ralphs, the supermarket. In restaurants. At the shopping mall. It was a bit surreal.

The first show aired on Monday, October 30, which just happened to be our wedding anniversary—*not* a coincidence. All our new friends came to the condo to watch the first show and to celebrate. The following day I checked my e-mails and found more than seventeen messages in my inbox. And even as I began to read through them, more e-mails kept arriving. *Ding! Ding! Ding!* The computer wouldn't stop dinging. I was asked to do a live Webchat on the Lifetime site after each show to answer questions. The message boards were so popular that the server couldn't cope with the response from the general public and it crashed! I had crashed Lifetime's server, I couldn't believe it!

Ray and Andrew called to say the numbers on the show had been great, and Lifetime was very excited!

"So am I!" I said.

Kev and I were overwhelmed. I didn't know where to turn. We had a bottle of champagne in the fridge, so Kev popped it open, and we sat down to reflect on how lucky we were to be in such a privileged position. Through my show I believed I would be able to bring some happiness into people's lives, either by connecting with the spirit of a loved one or by somehow providing inspiration and hope. What really matters is that I use my gift to bring peace and happiness to as many people as I can, and the show enables me to do that.

Early in December, however, with Christmas fast approaching, my thoughts turned to the New Year. We had been thinking about the future, but I knew that there were new horizons out there, and I felt it was time to move on. I had eighteen fantastic months with Lifetime, and the show had sold internationally, but I was beginning to miss the intimacy of my personal readings, which is where I got my start. Worse still, upward of thirty thousand people had written for advice, or to ask for readings, and my crazy schedule was making it impossible to get back to them. Television is pretty wonderful, certainly, but nothing beats the intimacy of human contact.

With the decision made, I began to book readings again, along with large audience events, and I finally started answering my e-mails—a digital mountain's worth of letters. If you've written, and I haven't gotten back to you, take heart—I'm working on it. Meanwhile, though, let me answer some of your most common questions:

Yes, I believe in life after death. When I say I am talking to a "spirit," I am referring to a person who has passed over to that other dimension, the Spirit Realm. I believe the Spirit Realm is sort of a weigh station. I've often compared it to one of those huge loading docks you see behind shopping malls or giant supermarkets. As soon as we pass over, all of us arrive at the same loading bay, where we are given an opportunity to reflect on our most recent life. The good we've done; the harm we may have caused; the mistakes we might have made. That done, we are whisked off to the appropriate department, which is based entirely on our actions and behaviors while we were alive. This is called *karma*, and, yes, I firmly believe in reincarnation. I believe that life is an endless cycle of birth and rebirth, and that it ends only when we've reached perfection.

On that happy final day, we reach the weigh station and discover that we're not going back. We've learned our lessons, we've lived a life wholly beyond reproach, so we're going all the way to the top, to the Head Office. Some people call this God, and some call it The Source, but there is no shortage of names for it: Yahweh, Allah, and Buddha are but three examples. But the name doesn't matter, since we're all talking about the same thing. When we reach that place, whatever we call it, we have reached the end of a very long journey, and it's the reward for a life—or, more accurately, *many* lives—well lived.

You will stumble along the way, certainly, and you will fall, but you must brush yourself off and be determined. And remember this: You don't have to do it alone. Look. Listen. Reach out. The Spirits are all around you, helping, guiding.

All you have to do is open your eyes.

Acknowledgments

I thank the two "boys" in my life, Charlie, and my husband, Kev.

Charlie, my little angel: You are the most precious thing in my life and every day you make my life worth living. You make me laugh and cry and you fill my world with joy. I never imagined I could love anyone as much as I love you. God bless you, my love. "Who's Mommy's special boy?"

Kev: Since you came into our lives you have worshipped and loved us both, and I couldn't ask for anything more. You have enough strength for us all and you make everything all right. You embrace our journey and my gift, and you understand that you have to share me with others who need healing. But you are the one who heals me unconditionally. I love you!

I thank my family:

Mom and Dad: You were always strong and you were there

to pick up the pieces. I could always rely on you both. Mom, you may not know this, but you kept me on my toes when it came to my "work"—you made me always try to honor and live up to Nan's legacy. I hope I'm getting there. Thanks for supporting me and coming to the shows and trying to convince Dad to come too. Dad, you taught me to acknowledge that we are all entitled to our own points of view, and that the world would be a pretty boring place if we were all the same!

Christian: Well, I know it took a lot of convincing, but I was so happy to see you at one of my shows. I'm not sure that makes you a believer, but your skepticism made me work harder, and as a result I always put everything into my work. Thank you for that!

Nan and Granddad: I can't thank you enough for everything you have done for me in your life. And Granddad, thank you for being Charlie's guardian angel!

Janey: You have been there for me when the times were really tough, and I feel that we stood together like sisters on the pathway of our intersecting lives. But when I think back, what I mostly remember is all the fun we had! Your friendship means the world to me, and you need to know that I will always be there for you, no matter where life takes us. I miss you! I thank you for your honesty, love, and support, but most of all for introducing me to the delights of champagne. Love you, chick!

Mike and Jonesy: You were the rock that Charlie and I went to for support so many times! We haven't forgotten that, and we never will. Your love and support shone through and made sure that we were safe. Jonesy, your levelheadedness and honesty got us through some of the toughest times of my life, and rest assured that Charlie will always be your "Monkey." Despite the many miles that separate us, you will always be close to our hearts. Love you, babes.

Nykki: Thanks for the walks, the chats, the friendship—and thanks especially for kicking my butt when I needed it. We are so proud of you and the journey that you are on. You will always be part of our family!

Sam "Mampa": You always believed in my gift, even when *I* didn't want to. Even when it scared you, you taught me that I had nothing to fear. You will always be special to me, and life will continue to bring us back together, so I know we will never be apart.

Rob and Raven: Thank you for helping us and guiding us in so many ways. It feels like we've known you for a lifetime and perhaps we have!

I also thank my many friends:

Anita, Denny, Richard, Chris & Linzi, Frankie, Elaine, Dick, Donnie, Stacee, Jodi, Joleen, Rebecca, Tanya, Melanie in South Africa. You have all touched us in so many ways and we are so glad you are in our lives. This recent journey would not have been so easy if it wasn't for you guys, so thank you!

Simon, Louise, and Daisy: I know we have had our ups and downs, but sometimes you go through these before you find that neutral space where everyone can work together—and I believe we've finally found it. Thank you for loving Charlie the way that you do, which means so much to us all. Thank you for supporting us on this journey, and for not standing in my way, even when it meant missing Charlie. He loves you and misses you, too. Thank you!

Thanks to everyone at Merv Griffin Entertainment, for believing in me and for the care and integrity with which you produced the show. A special thanks to Dallas, for being there for me during those endless early days, and for tirelessly reminding me that my life was about to go though a huge change. (Well, you were right!)

Ray Brune: "I promise I won't #@*# it up!" Andrew Yani: "Yes, I know I'm part of the family!" I will never forget New York City, where it all started, and I often look back and marvel at how far we've come. It's been great to share this incredible journey with you guys!

Yann: You and Susan are absolutely wonderful. We are so happy to have you in our lives and want to thank you again for creating an amazing show.

To the incredible crew who worked on *Life Among the Dead*: You came back for more thrills on the second series, which made me wonder: *Are you crazy?!* I love you guys. A special thanks to Rob Scott, for your tireless support—and for all the hugs. Scotty I miss turning around and not finding you in my face. Thanks also to Jilly, Sharon, and Stef—the Glam Squad. You girlies are just fabulous! And one more thanks to Bob, Paulie, and Chris, for just being you! Top Banana!

My heartfelt thanks to the executives at Lifetime, who took a chance on me. I love being part of the Lifetime family!

Thanks to Tricia Boczkowski, my editor at Simon Spotlight Entertainment, who always guided me with a steady hand, and who has been my biggest fan from day one; and to Mel Berger, who was instrumental in making this deal happen.

Thanks also to Pablo Fenjves, without whose help I couldn't have written this book. I felt so at home at your place, sitting in that comfy corner chair and pouring out my heart, and I want to thank you for your patience, for making the process so much fun, and especially for all the laughs. You are my friendly "ghost"!

Thanks also to you, the reader, for reading my story, for watching the show, and for believing in me. You are the reason I am able to share this gift, and I am forever grateful.

About the Author

Born in Birmingham, England, Lisa Williams makes her home in Los Angeles as well as in the small town of Redditch in picturesque Worcestershire. She lives with her husband, Kevin, and nine-year-old son, Charlie, who, according to his mom, has already shown an inherited gift for natural healing and talking with spirits.

Notes

Notes

Hay House Titles of Related Interest

YOU CAN HEAL YOUR LIFE, the movie,
starring Louise L. Hay & Friends
(available as a 1-DVD set and an expanded 2-DVD set)
Watch the trailer at www.LouiseHayMovie.com

❊ ❊ ❊ ❊

Ask & It Is Given,
by Esther and Jerry Hicks

Crossing Over,
by John Edward

David Wells' Complete Guide to Developing Your Psychic Skills,
by David Wells

Developing Mediumship,
by Gordon Smith

Why My Mother Didn't Want Me to Be Psychic,
by Heidi Sawyer

We hope you enjoyed this Hay House book.
If you would like to receive a free catalogue featuring additional
Hay House books and products, or if you would like information
about the Hay Foundation, please contact:

Hay House UK Ltd
292B Kensal Rd • London W10 5BE
Tel: (44) 20 8962 1230; Fax: (44) 20 8962 1239
www.hayhouse.co.uk

***

Published and distributed in the United States of America by:
Hay House, Inc. • PO Box 5100 • Carlsbad, CA 92018-5100
Tel.: (1) 760 431 7695 or (1) 800 654 5126;
Fax: (1) 760 431 6948 or (1) 800 650 5115
www.hayhouse.com

Published and distributed in Australia by:
Hay House Australia Ltd • 18/36 Ralph St • Alexandria NSW 2015
Tel.: (61) 2 9669 4299; Fax: (61) 2 9669 4144
www.hayhouse.com.au

Published and distributed in the Republic of South Africa by:
Hay House SA (Pty) Ltd • PO Box 990 • Witkoppen 2068
Tel./Fax: (27) 11 467 8904 • www.hayhouse.co.za

Published and distributed in India by:
Hay House Publishers India • Muskaan Complex • Plot No.3
B-2 • Vasant Kunj • New Delhi – 110 070.
Tel.: (91) 11 41761620; Fax: (91) 11 41761630.
www.hayhouse.co.in

Distributed in Canada by:
Raincoast • 9050 Shaughnessy St • Vancouver, BC V6P 6E5
Tel.: (1) 604 323 7100; Fax: (1) 604 323 2600

***

Sign up via the Hay House UK website to receive the Hay House
online newsletter and stay informed about what's going on with
your favourite authors. You'll receive bimonthly announcements
about discounts and offers, special events, product highlights,
free excerpts, giveaways, and more!
www.hayhouse.co.uk

JOIN THE HAY HOUSE FAMILY

As the leading self-help, mind, body and spirit publisher in the UK, we'd like to welcome you to our family so that you can enjoy all the benefits our website has to offer.

 EXTRACTS from a selection of your favourite author titles

 COMPETITIONS, PRIZES & SPECIAL OFFERS Win extracts, money off, downloads and so much more

 LISTEN to a range of radio interviews and our latest audio publications

 CELEBRATE YOUR BIRTHDAY An inspiring gift will be sent your way

 LATEST NEWS Keep up with the latest news from and about our Authors

 ATTEND OUR AUTHOR EVENTS Be the first to hear about our author events

 iPHONE APPS Download your favourite app for your iPhone

 HAY HOUSE INFORMATION Ask us anything, all enquiries answered

join us online at **www.hayhouse.co.uk**

 292B Kensal Road, London W10 5BE
T: 020 8962 1230 E: info@hayhouse.co.uk